MW00573200

Sid Diqui is My Friend

A MEMOIR

Sid Diqui is My Friend

Sid or Siddiqui, the name given to illicit
alcohol in Saudi Arabia

**A behind-the-scenes look at life, working
for the largest oil company in the world; or
for some, how greed and arrogance can lead
to imprisonment**

Mark Carlile

First Published in 2014 by Michael G. Coates, Publishing. British Columbia, Canada

Copyright © Michael G Coates 2014
Copyright Registration Number 1112323
All rights reserved. No part of this publication may be reproduced, stored in a retrieval system, or transmitted, in any form or by any means, electronic, mechanical, photocopying, recording, or otherwise, without the written prior permission of the author.

ISBN: 978-0-9937154-0-2

Printed by CreateSpace, an Amazon.com Company

Available from book stores, and online book retailers, including:

Amazon.com
Amazon Europe
Amazon.ca
CreateSpace Direct
CreateSpace eStore
Barnes & Noble
Ingram
NACSCORP

Available as an e-book at:

Amazon.com
Amazon Kindle Store
Apple i Bookstore
Kobobooks.com
bn.com

Contents

About the Author

Mark Carlile was born in 1941 during the Second World War, and grew up in rural England. His mother died just after he was born.

His grandmother and her three daughters were evacuated from Sussex to Devon because of the war. He lived on a farm with them and his cousin, Noreen, until the war ended. His father returned from the war in 1946.

At age sixteen, Mark left home to serve a five-year apprenticeship as a toolmaker with Westland Aircraft in Yeovil, Somerset.

He immigrated to Canada in 1968. In Canada, he first worked as an engineering inspector with a company in Calgary that manufactured track vehicles for the oil industry.

For the next seven years Mark worked in various engineering positions. In 1975 he was hired by Monenco Inc. in Calgary as an engineering inspector and promoted to inspection supervisor. In this position he was primarily responsible for the inspection and testing of large electrical control panels for power stations and high voltage switchgear for companies

such as Calgary Power, Saskatchewan Power, Hydro Quebec, and Syncrude Canada Ltd.

It was while working with Monenco Inc. that Mark was hired by the Arabian American Oil Company (Aramco) to work in Saudi Arabia.

Following his return to Canada in 1985, he formed a company that designed and manufactured pneumatic actuators for the oil industry. He also worked for a petrochemical company for 15 years as director of quality assurance. Mark retired in 2003 and now lives in British Columbia, Canada.

He was inspired to write 'Sid Diqui is my Friend' because friends enjoyed the many interesting stories he told about his life while working in Saudi Arabia.

Dedication

This book is dedicated to my grandmother on my father's side. Without her love, support and dedication in seeing that I had a good start in life, I may not have followed a successful career path.

It is also dedicated to all the people who have been afflicted with a condition known as Myositis. I'm confident that one day research will be able to find the reason for this condition, and also find a cure.

Acknowledgements

The cover of this book was developed from an oil painting, by Mr Seong-Bae Kim (김승배), which I purchased in Al-Khobar, Saudi Arabia, in 1984.
A resident in Saudi Arabia for many years and an artist of repute, Mr Seong-Bae Kim is the gallery manager for the Faisal Art Gallery in Al-Khobar, and owner of the Kim.Art Gallery in Al-Khobar.
Mr Kim can be contacted at PO box 2810, Al-Khobar 31952, Saudi Arabia. sbkim48@hanmail.net.
Thank you Mr Kim for allowing me to use your artwork.

Many thanks to Sandra Morton for the generous donation of her time in editing the drafts of this book, and correcting numerous errors in spelling, grammar, punctuation, style and usage.

Finally, a special thanks to my wife for proofreading, checking, guidance and support in the writing of the drafts of this book.

People in this book

The names of people in this book have been changed to protect their privacy.

Austin Barton	Work associate. VID
Beth Somerton	Work associate. DPD
Blaine Carlile	Son of Monica and Mark Carlile
Chandra	Secretary for VID
Daren Leman	Work associate. VID
Dave Hansen	Inspection supervisor. VID
Dennis McBride	Work associate. Servog
Evan and Jamie Baynes	Daycare owners. Daughter Shane
Floyd Harper	Work associate. VID
Frazer and Kim	Friends in Dhahran. Children Cinda and Josh.
Ganesh Kumar	Plant manager

Garth and Danielle Fenton	Friends. Children Garth Junior and James
Garth Rhymer	Al-Qahtani Laboratory
George Dennison	Plant manager of a coatings company
Gerry Morrow	Work associate. VID
James and Janet O'Leary	Friends in Dhahran
James Henderson	Al-Qahtani QA
Jane	Mark's daughter from his previous marriage
Jim and Annette DeAngelo	Friends. Jim worked with Mark
Jim McColl	Mark's diving buddy
John Calmar	Monica's supervisor at the Dhahran hospital
Lorna Barton	Austin Barton's wife
Lorne Isborne	Work associate. VID
Mark Carlile	The author
Monica Carlile	Wife of Mark Carlile
Pat and Colette Miller	Friends. Daughters Alana and Sarah
Porter Danton	Personnel manager and next-door neighbour
Roger Morgan	A longtime friend in Calgary
Robin Parker	Work associate. VID
Ron and Dee Wilmingdon	Friends from Calgary
Shirley and Bill	Friends in Ras Tanura
Steve Carmichael	Work associate. VID
Ted and Linda Griffin	Friends. Daughters Lorna and Annette

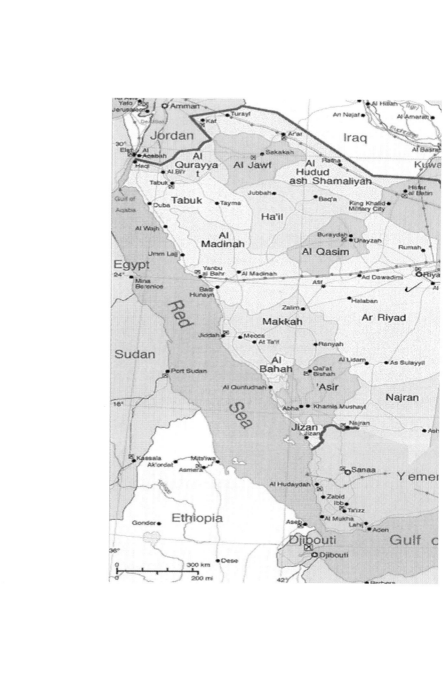

Iran

Deztul
Estahan
Yazd
Ahvaz
Bandar-e
Khomeyni
Abadan
Kerman
Zahedan
Kuwait
Shiraz
Sa'idabad
Ra's al Khafji
Bandar-e
Bushehr
PERSIAN GULF
Bandar-e Abbas
Al Jubayl
Ad Dammam
Dhahran
Bahrain
Manama
Ra's al Khaymah
Oman
Qatar
Doha
Dubayy
Gulf of
Oman
Al
Huluf
Abu Dhabi
Al Fujayrah
Suhar
As Salwa
Al
Buraymi
Muscat
Harad
United Arab
Emirates
Sur

ARABIAN
SEA

Boundary Undefined

Ash Sharaqiyah
Oman
60°

Boundary Undefined

Sharawrah
Salalah

Saudi Arabia		
⊙	National Capital	
•	City	
⊠	Airfields	
⊙——⊙	Crude Oil Pipeline	
	Primary Road	
	Railroad	
– – – –	1967 Cease Fire Line	
	1949 Armistice Line	
	Emirate Border	
	International Border	
– – –	Administrative Line	

Saywun
Al Mukalla
Sayhut
Arabian

Aden
Sea

Somalia
48°
54°

CHAPTER 1

Overseas Employment

It was a warm spring day on Calgary's 9th Avenue, as Roger and I went for a lunch-time stroll. We wanted to get some fresh air and a little exercise, after spending the morning at our office desks at the engineering consulting firm of Monenco Inc. There was still a cool nip in the air, but the midday sun felt warm and inviting as we walked along 9th Avenue SW, between 2nd and 4th Street.

Roger Morgan and I were longtime friends and were both employed as inspection engineers for this international firm of consultants. Roger and I emigrated from the United Kingdom after having worked in the aircraft industry for many years in the South West part of England in a little town called Yeovil, in the county of Somerset. We both had completed a five-year apprenticeship with Westland Aircraft Ltd., a manufacturer of helicopters. We both decided there were more opportunities in Canada, and more money to be made by leaving England. I emigrated in 1968, and Roger in 1975. I was an inspection supervisor for Monenco Inc. We hired Roger in 1977 when work became hard to get in Port Alberni on Vancouver Island, where Roger initially sought his fortune.

As we wandered along 9th Avenue, Roger noticed a flyer in the office window of an employment agency. It expounded on the large salaries and travel opportunities available working overseas in the oil industry.

"Why don't we look into that," Roger said.

We climbed the stairway to the second-floor office of the employment agency, and walked through the open door into a sparsely furnished office. We were greeted by a tall man with a handlebar moustache who stood up from his desk as we entered.

"You guys interested in work overseas?" he asked. "If you're in the oil industry, I probably have a job for you."

Within a few minutes we were both collecting application forms for work in Saudi Arabia for the oil giant Aramco.

We returned the forms to the employment agency the following week. After not hearing anything for a month, Roger and I decided it was a lost cause.

My wife Monica was six months pregnant with her first child when a letter arrived from Houston, Texas. We were both invited for an interview with Aramco in the company's Houston offices. The letter said that a four-day interview and orientation had been arranged for us in Houston. Following our confirmation of the travel date in the letter, airline tickets would be booked in our names and a hotel reservation would be made for us at the company hotel.

I immediately contacted Roger to see if he had received a similar invitation.

"I've not received anything yet," Roger said. "But if you had a reply, I expect I'll get a letter in a few days." "Keep your fingers crossed, buddy!"

We had a good flight to Houston, changing planes in Chicago. As we waited at the baggage carousel at the Houston airport to collect our bags, my heart sank when the carousel came to a stop. Everyone collecting bags had left, and our bags hadn't arrived. I had visions of going to an interview with Aramco, dressed in blue jeans and a T-shirt. When we reported the missing baggage, it was discovered our bags had been routed through Dallas/Fort Worth. Approximately an hour later, our bags arrived in Houston. With the security measures in place today this couldn't happen, as all baggage has to accompany a passenger. All's well that ends well.

It was a hot June day when Monica and I arrived in Houston. The humidity was high—not something we were used to. When we exited our hotel for the taxi ride to the Aramco offices, it was like walking into a sauna. It was our first trip to Houston and the Lone Star State.

While I was being interviewed for my job with Aramco, Monica, along with a group of wives of the other men who were being interviewed, was given a brief orientation on life in Saudi Arabia. At noontime, everyone was taken to a large conference room where lunch had been catered by a local restaurant.

Life in Saudi Arabia was the topic of conversation during the 90-minute lunch. Several Aramco employees who had lived or visited the Aramco compounds in Saudi Arabia, were on hand to advise the potential employees on living and working in the Middle East.

"How did your morning go?" I asked Monica.

"It was interesting," she replied. "They showed us a movie on Dhahran and a slide presentation showing pictures of the various camps and facilities available in each camp."

After lunch, I attended more interviews for a job as an inspector with Aramco's Vendor Inspection Division in Dhahran. I advised the interviewer that in my present position with Monenco Inc. I was responsible for the inspection and testing of large control panels, as well as electrical distribution panels, instrumentation for the oil industry, and high voltage switchgear for mining. The interviewer was shown photographs of some of the equipment I had been involved with during the past few years. I assumed that if I was offered a job with Aramco, I would be involved with instrumentation and electrical equipment. This was my main area of expertise. The interviewer seemed impressed with my qualifications and experience. He advised me that during the next three days my wife and I would be given an in-depth orientation in preparation for our life in Saudi Arabia in an Aramco compound.

"If you have any questions during the orientation, don't be afraid to ask," he told me. "We're here to answer all the questions you may have."

The Aramco orientation process is very informative: outlining all the facilities, living conditions and way of life in the Aramco compounds. During the three-day orientation, people who had lived, worked or visited the Aramco compounds in Saudi Arabia gave numerous presentations. They shared tales of their experiences, working and living conditions and, sometimes, frustrations in a country that's foreign to most people. They described a slower pace of life to that of North America. How the country is under-developed and has little in the way of infrastructure and amenities to what most North Americans are used to.

One presenter told the story about his trip from Dhahran to Ras Tanura along a twisty two-lane highway across the desert landscape. As they drove their car toward a railroad crossing with a train approaching, they came to a stop to allow the train to pass. Very quickly, Saudi drivers in large sedans and pick-up trucks parked alongside them on both sides. They formed a line six to eight vehicles wide and parking in the oncoming lane as well as in the desert beside the road. When the train cleared the track, he saw a similar line had formed on the opposite side of the track.

"It was chaos for a few minutes," he said, "as vehicles shuffled around one another with horns blasting in frustration and hands waving out of vehicle windows. Eventually it all sorted itself out and everyone went on their way."

I thought this was a bit of an exaggeration. I had a hard time believing that something like this could actually happen.

Aramco's orientation program provided a good overview of the lifestyle we could expect while living in Dhahran, and the restrictions we would encounter living in Saudi Arabia.

Dhahran has its own golf course, two swimming pools, beach, yacht club, riding stables, library and woodworking shop. Other Aramco compounds throughout Saudi Arabia have some facilities, but not to the extent of Dhahran, which is the central hub for engineering activities.

Because Aramco had a housing shortage at the current time, we were advised some new hires will live in local communities. Sea View, a condo complex on the beach at Al-Khobar a drive of about 30 minutes' from Dhahran, was being used to house some new hires.

Aramco did a thorough job of its orientation program, and left no questions unanswered, even though there were many. I hadn't been offered a job with Aramco following my interviews. It appeared that Aramco considers it worthwhile to go through a basic orientation during the hiring process. It is more cost-effective for a potential hire to decide it is not for him and his wife at this stage, rather than when they get to Saudi Arabia along with their belongings.

During our trip back to our hotel following the second day of orientation, we shared a taxi with another couple from Calgary, Ron and Dee Wilmingdon. Ron was also being interviewed for a position with Aramco. Ron, a geophysicist with Imperial Oil, was being seconded to Aramco for a two-year period just prior to his retirement at age 65. Monica and I didn't realize it at the time, but they would become good friends when we all arrived in Saudi Arabia. Ron would later be sent back to Canada for a social misconduct that Aramco didn't tolerate.

During the flight back to Calgary, Monica and I wondered if this was the right thing for us, especially with a baby on the way. It was a good opportunity for me, and would provide a substantial increase in salary and the possibility of tax-free status as a non-resident of Canada. Monica was working as a physiotherapist in a private clinic in Calgary, which would mean her giving up work. However, Aramco had indicated that it might be possible for her to get a job as a physiotherapist in the Dhahran Hospital, when she was ready. They couldn't offer her a job or make a commitment until we were both in Saudi Arabia.

8   SID DIQUI IS MY FRIEND

CHAPTER 2

The Job Offer

Monica gave birth to a healthy baby boy on August 29, named Blaine. At that time I hadn't received a job offer from Aramco. A week or two later I received a package from Aramco. It contained instructions on packing air and sea shipments for our trip to Saudi Arabia, along with inventory forms that had to be completed in triplicate.

I didn't understand this as I hadn't received a job offer from Aramco or received any other correspondence from Houston.

When I contacted Aramco in Houston, they said probably shipping had gotten ahead of job placement, and I would receive an offer of employment in the near future. The job offer came by courier a week later. I was a little disappointed because the salary was lower than I had anticipated. When I analyzed it closely, I realized that with benefits, overseas hardship allowance and tax-free status, I would nearly double my present salary. I contacted Aramco and accepted the position as inspector in Aramco's Vendor Inspection Division in Dhahran.

I was qualified as an instrumentation technician, and had been working on instrumentation and electrical equipment with Monenco Inc. for the past four years. As far as I knew, I would be working in a similar capacity in Saudi Arabia.

When I met Roger at the office on the following Monday, he hadn't received a word from his application to Aramco. At this point, Roger considered his application a dead issue. I had had visions of the two of us working together again in the Middle East, but it wasn't to be. I wondered if my status as supervisor had any bearing on my job offer. I later discovered that many of my North American work associates in my office in Saudi Arabia, had also held supervisory or managerial positions prior to working for Aramco.

Blaine gave Monica and me a few sleepless nights, but by and large he was a satisfied baby and was soon sleeping through the night. His blond hair, hazel eyes and loving smile captivated the ladies. When Monica and I visited the Philippines during one of our later vacations, he was an instant hit with the girls. He was very little trouble during his first few months, and seemed to take a liking to people. During the next few years Blaine would travel the world and his businessman's passport became clogged with stamps. Unfortunately, he would remember little of his adventures.

I realized that being near the Red Sea, I would have a wonderful opportunity to take advantage of some of the best diving in the world. However, I hadn't done any scuba diving and had no qualifications for this sport.

I enrolled in a basic scuba diving class in Calgary, and during the next few weeks took classroom and pool training. This was followed by an open-water dive in early October in the frigid waters of Lake Minnewanka in the mountains west of Calgary. Although I had a wetsuit on, the cold, deep lake took my breath away when I entered the water. The water temperature was two degrees Celsius. I completed my basic certification with the National Association of Scuba Diving Schools (NASDS).

Monica and I completed the inventory forms for an 80-cubic-foot air shipment container, which would arrive in Dhahran before we did. Aramco supplied the container, which Monica and I packed ourselves. Every item had to be described in detail, and valued. Aramco advised us not to use company names in their descriptions. They advised that if the company name had a Jewish connection, the Arabian customs officials would confiscate the item. Aramco wasn't allowed to provide a list of those companies. Likewise, they recommended we remove company names (if possible) from items in our shipment.

After the air shipment was completed and dispatched, a sea shipment was prepared. Aramco is very generous when it comes to shipping your belongings by sea. Virtually anything can be shipped, including furniture and appliances, and Aramco covers the cost. We only shipped essential items, including Blaine's toys.

We had arranged to rent our house to a friend whilst we were away, and would be storing our furniture in the basement of our home. Nevertheless, our sea shipment did consist of several large boxes containing sports equipment, clothing and kitchen equipment. We wouldn't need furniture when we initially arrived in Arabia, as we would be staying in furnished accommodation until we were assigned housing in Dhahran. (Later when we were assigned housing in Dhahran, we decided that we would rent furniture and appliances from Aramco).

The Aramco coordinator advised me that another couple, Ted and Linda Griffin, had also been hired from Calgary, and would most probably travel to Saudi Arabia at the same time. Monica invited Ted and Linda over for drinks one evening. We learned that Ted would be working on computers in the exploration department of Aramco. They had two girls: Lorna two years old and Annette three months. They were both looking forward to living in Saudi Arabia. Linda's parents, however, weren't excited about them leaving Canada.

I sold my beloved 1968 E Type Jaguar and used the money to pay off part of the mortgage on our home. It was my pride and joy, but we didn't know how long we would be away. Storage charges would mount up if we were gone for several years. In addition, to become a non-resident for tax purposes you couldn't own a car, and had to either sell property or rent it on a long-term lease. Monica's Datsun 610 was also sold, and we kept our Chrysler Cordoba until a few days before we left Canada.

JOURNEY TO THE MIDDLE EAST   13

CHAPTER 3

Journey to the Middle East

Aramco made arrangements for Monica and me to fly to Houston just after Christmas. We would stay there for four days to go through further orientation programs, and would be assigned our temporary housing.

For the trip to Houston, Monica packed two large suitcases and a trunk containing clothing and baby apparel. I intended to buy a scuba tank and diving regulators in Houston, so room was left in the trunk for this equipment.

Our flight to Houston required a change of planes in Chicago, and was an uneventful trip. We took a shuttle bus from the airport to the Stouffer's hotel, which was near the Aramco offices. The hotel was booked and paid for by Aramco, and all meals were included. However, we were responsible for our mini-bar bill!

The next day (Monday) we took a taxi to the Aramco offices to attend the new hire orientation program. Blaine, who was then four months old, also attended.

We were apprised of the cultural differences we could expect, along with dress attire for both men and women. Monica was advised not to wear tight-fitting clothing, and to cover her head with a scarf when she was in a public place away from the Aramco compounds. She was also advised that she would only be allowed to drive a car in the Aramco compounds. Even Saudi women aren't allowed to drive a motor vehicle; their husband or a driver has to drive them wherever they need to go.

Dhahran, (Camp or Main Camp, as it is often referred to) has its own commissary where basic food supplies can be purchased. It also has a post office, bank and hairdressing salon. All kinds of products are available from the Aramco special order sales catalogue. If there is no listing for a product, Aramco will do its best to get it for you.

There is a large hospital in Dhahran, which is staffed mostly by American, Canadian, British and Filipino personnel. It is equipped to handle most routine medical conditions and procedures. Those who need major surgery procedures are air evacuated to either the United States or the King Faisal Hospital in Riyadh. Medical treatment is free to Aramco personnel.

Housing assignment works on a points system, which is something we weren't made aware of when I initially accepted the overseas position. Employees are given a grade code, which gives them an allotment of points towards temporary and permanent housing. I was assigned grade code 11. The higher your grade code, the more points you accumulate, and the quicker you get into Main Camp housing. Points also accumulate with time served with Aramco. Housing assignment is also on a bidding process.

We were assigned a condo unit at Sea View. It is serviced by an Aramco Greyhound bus to provide transportation to Dhahran or Al Khobar for the wives and children. The service runs about every two hours, and the bus is rarely crowded.

The three-day orientation covered many topics about conditions in the Middle East. It included Aramco housing and facilities, travel and transportation, buying a car, what to expect at the airport, annual repatriation, dress code, banking, shipment of furniture, health and safety, alcohol regulations and do's and don'ts in a foreign country, and many other topics.

Alcohol is not allowed into Saudi Arabia, and they cautioned everyone not to attempt to conceal alcohol on their person or in luggage. If found, Aramco wouldn't be able to help us, as it is a very serious offence and could result in a prison sentence.

We were also informed that Saudi customs officials at the airport are very thorough, and frequently empty all the contents of a suitcase onto the counter during their search. When they're finished, they expect the owner to repack their suitcase. This is sometimes difficult as everything becomes a colossal mess. Clothes are left unfolded and in a heap, making it almost impossible to get them back into the suitcase.

Aramco did its best to ensure that new hires have no real surprises when they land in Saudi Arabia. We were impressed with the thoroughness of the orientation program.

I was advised that a representative from my department would meet us at the airport and provide transportation to our condo at Sea View. We would arrive on a Friday, and as Thursday and Friday is the weekend in Saudi Arabia, I was expected to report for work on Saturday morning at seven.

I took a taxi to a local diving shop during our stay in Houston, and bought a scuba tank, regulators, fins and a mask. I was advised that the tank should be drained of air just before departure, as a full tank shouldn't be taken on board an aircraft. I was also advised to refill the tank as soon as possible after arriving in Arabia. When I returned to the hotel, we packed the tank at the bottom of the hard-sided trunk along with the regulators. We put baby clothing, and about three dozen diapers on the top to fill the trunk. I anticipated the Saudi customs officials would probably see the baby provisions and not investigate further when they searched our baggage. It is not illegal to take diving equipment into Arabia, but I preferred they didn't find it. Just before we left our hotel for the airport, I reached into the trunk and drained all the air from the tank as instructed.

Aramco has its own fleet of aircraft, and was using a specially equipped Boeing aircraft to fly personnel to Saudi Arabia. All the seating in this aircraft is first class, similar to the first-class seating found in a commercial passenger airliner. The flight is a direct flight from Houston to Dhahran, making one stop in Paris to refuel.

We met Ted and Linda Griffin again at the orientation, and found that we would all be travelling on the same aircraft to Arabia. Ted and Linda would also be housed in Sea View.

Monica, Blaine and I were seated on the Aramco Boeing aircraft at the Houston airport at approximately 4:00 p.m. The flight was full and took off on schedule. In addition to new hires, there were people on board who were flying to Dhahran for meetings. There were also drilling personnel who work on a rotating shift of 28 days on and 28 days off. When we were airborne, the pilot indicated that the flight crew would be serving supper, and reminded all on board that the service of alcoholic beverages would cease immediately when we were over Saudi Arabian air space.

Lots of drinking time left yet, I thought.

Service and food on the Aramco aircraft matched the seating (first class), and all beverages were free.

"Make the most of it," said one of the passengers across the aisle from me. "You'll not see a decent drink again until you leave Arabia."

The Aramco Boeing landed at Paris Charles de Gaulle Airport and everyone deplaned whilst the aircraft was refuelled. It was good to stretch and walk around for a while after the six-hour flight to Europe. After about an hour, we were back on board. Our flight was soon gaining momentum down the runway, and airborne en route to Dhahran. After another movie, breakfast and lunch, we were well on our way to the Middle East.

We really appreciated first-class as the seats were much larger than regular seating, and the space between the seats provided lots of legroom. The seats almost fully reclined which made it possible to get some reasonable sleep.

When I got up to go to the washroom at the rear of the aircraft, I met three roughnecks who were returning to their oil rig after 28 days off. They were standing by the aircraft galley and were into a bottle of Jack Daniels. It had been left with them by a stewardess. I enjoyed their company, stories about Arabia and the Jack Daniels. However, I decided that I should return

to my seat and get reasonably sober before arriving at
our destination. I didn't want to get off the aircraft
drunk or smelling of alcohol. A few hours later, the
stewardess announced we were now in Saudi air space
and alcoholic beverages would no longer be available.

Sand and low mountains were the only terrain
visible from the port side of the aircraft. I noticed the
horizon was a blur of brown dust where the sky met the
desert floor.

The aircraft arrived at Dhahran Airport at
approximately 6:00 p.m. on Friday, and all passengers
disembarked onto the tarmac. We were escorted into
the airport building by Saudi officials. After a long wait,
we were reunited with our luggage, and were told to
proceed to the customs area. During our orientation,
Aramco advised us it is sometimes worthwhile to get a
porter to assist with taking luggage through customs.
You have to pay them 40 to 50 riyals. It is worth it, as
the porter can speak Arabic and has an interest in
getting you through the customs area as quickly as
possible. He'll also lift your heavy cases onto the
counter. The customs people also seem to look kindly
on the fact that you're helping to support and provide
work for a fellow countryman.

Monica, Blaine and I proceeded to the customs area
assisted by a porter, and were shocked to see the chaos
at the customs counters. There appeared to be no
organization at all. Hundreds of people, some with
families, of many nationalities tried to push their way
to the customs counters to have their baggage cleared.
It was a total free-for-all, with no resemblance of a
lineup. You push and shove your way to the counter
assisted by the porter. He appeared to be accustomed
to this kind of disorganization.

The customs area consisted of a long line of countertops, where Saudi custom officials searched every bag and container that was placed on the counter. Sometimes, they pulled out all the contents for examination. Afterwards, they just left everything on the counter or in a heap on top of the bag for the owner to repack. When they were satisfied, they placed a chalk mark on the bag. Monica and I finally made our way to the counter where the porter placed the first bag for inspection.

The customs official pulled out some of our clothing with a cursory examination. He then proceeded to search through the bag with his hands and disrupted the organized packing. The case wouldn't close again! After he had finished and had placed his customary chalk mark on the bag, he proceeded to the next bag that the porter had placed on the countertop. I took Blaine whilst Monica tried to repack the case. She eventually got everything back in sufficiently to allow the zipper to close. After the same procedure with the second case, the customs official opened the trunk that contained my scuba tank and equipment. The top third part of the trunk was full of baby clothes, and on the very top were three or four layers of diapers. The official scoffed at the diapers, throwing a few of them into the air, apparently puzzled as to why someone would bring diapers into the country. He didn't venture into the trunk at all, as he probably concluded that it was full of baby apparel. Shaking his head he mumbled something and placed a chalk mark on the trunk. Monica refastened the trunk, and the porter proceeded to the exit with our luggage.

Near the exit there was another customs official whose job was to look at every bag and find the customary chalk mark that signified the bag had indeed been checked. The passenger could then proceed to the exit. After all three bags were checked, we were cleared to proceed. We made our way through to the exit with our baggage on a cart pushed by the porter.

Immediately outside the customs area, a line of people greeted us. Many had signs and placards with names looking for passengers and new arrivals whom they didn't know by face recognition. I quickly spotted my name on a card being waved by a man in his early forties. He was dressed in blue jeans with a big oval western belt buckle and a western shirt. He had a weather-beaten suntanned complexion, and I thought the only thing that was missing was his horse.

"Hi Mark," came the greeting from the man with a broad Texas accent. "I'm here to pick you up and take you to your accommodation in Sea View."

He introduced himself as Jim DeAngelo. His wife Annette, who's French Canadian, accompanied him.

I tipped the porter with the customary 50 riyals, and the porter said "shukran" and departed for the terminal and his next customer.

CHAPTER 4

Sea View, Our New Home

Annette took Blaine and gave him a hug and cuddle, whilst Jim and I carried the luggage to Jim's Plymouth sedan, which was parked by the curbside.

It was about 21 degrees Celsius (70 degrees Fahrenheit) at Dhahran airport, with a light breeze and evidence of a recent rainfall on the airport roadway. We were soon on our way out of the airport terminal, and headed for our new home in Sea View in the suburbs of Al-Khobar. The roadway we travelled on was tarmacked, but was broken and uneven in many places with frequent deep potholes that Jim managed to avoid. The desert on either side of the road was littered with discarded rubbish and the occasional wrecked car. As we approached the coastal area just north of Al-Khobar, we passed through a sparsely populated residential area with the occasional date palm blowing in the light sea breeze. Most of the homes were flat-roofed structures with architecture similar to that found in Mexico. Quite often, the homes were surrounded by a high wall with wrought-iron entry gates and gated driveways. There appeared to be no standard or restriction for building, as some homes were little more than shacks whilst others were obviously owned by the more wealthy Saudi Arabians.

I noticed that residential housing in the suburbs of Al-Khobar varied considerably. Some homes were built very close together. Others were adjacent to vacant land that sometimes resembled a garbage dump with rubbish strewn about the area amid piles of sand. Most of the homes were single-or two-storey structures, some next to what looked like ramshackle small businesses or shops.

Jim made a stop at the local Safeway supermarket on the way to Sea View, in case we needed any special foods for Blaine or other provisions. He advised us that Aramco had done some grocery shopping for us, and had stocked our refrigerator and larder with sufficient groceries so that we would have provisions for a couple of days.

A Safeway supermarket was the last thing we expected to find in Saudi Arabia. Annette took Blaine whilst Monica and I purchased a few previsions. Monica was very tired after our long flight, but took the opportunity to buy extra baby food, a few cans of vegetables and some bottled water.

As we approached the entrance to Sea View, a barrier arm blocked the entrance road. Our vehicle came to a stop and a guard stepped out from his security box to see who was approaching. He seemed to immediately recognize Jim DeAngelo and lifted the barrier so that we could pass.

The Sea View complex consisted of approximately forty white stucco condominiums with green and brown tile roofs. Each unit was two storeys with an arched balcony on the upper level that had black wrought-iron railings. Just inside the main entrance to the complex on the left were a tennis court and an inground swimming pool with no water in it. A high security wall surrounded the complex to keep out intruders.

Jim parked the car in front of our new home and advised us that his unit was close by in the complex. Jim and Annette helped carry our luggage into our new abode, and Annette said she'd baked us an apple pie that she would get for us in a few minutes. Jim advised me that as Saturday is a workday in Saudi Arabia, he would take me to work in the morning, leaving Sea View at six fifteen for the drive into Dhahran. Jim also said that casual clothing is the order of the day at the office, and that blue jeans or slacks and an open neck shirt was recognized as acceptable attire. Jim said that I should bring my passport as well as Monica's and Blaine's as they had to be turned into the passport office on camp. Jim and Annette then left us to unpack.

The condo was adequate for temporary accommodation, and was furnished with the essentials of daily living. A TV, stereo and cassette player were provided, as well as all the basic cutlery and culinary needs. The upper level consisted of a bathroom with shower, and two bedrooms with ample closet space for the clothing that Monica and I had brought with us. The master bedroom had a king size bed. A clock radio was also provided.

Probably Aramco considered that a clock radio was essential, I thought, as being on time for work was important to productivity.

Annette arrived with the pie and wished us bon appétit as she exited the sliding doors that were the main entrance to our unit.

After unpacking our clothes, Monica was exhausted, and lay down on the bed for a nap. I entertained Blaine downstairs whilst Monica slept. I tried to get a TV station, but only found one Arabic channel, but the reception was very poor. I later found that Aramco had its own TV channel, but it only broadcasted from 4:00 to 10:00 p.m.

After half an hour of shuteye, Monica came downstairs and made some supper for us. The daylight was starting to fade, and I noticed that it got dark very quickly, much quicker than back home.

Our biological clocks were all out of kilter after the long flight to the Middle East. But sleep that night came easily due to the lack of adequate rest on the flight to Dhahran.

CHAPTER 5

The First Day

We were awake early Saturday morning before the alarm sounded on the clock radio. I had showered and had a light breakfast long before six. I was ready for the trip to Dhahran when Jim rapped on the door at our departure time of six fifteen. Blaine was still in bed and asleep when I left for my first day of work, and Monica took the opportunity to get some more rest before Blaine started his day in his new surroundings.

It was still dark when Jim and I left Sea View for the trip to Main Camp in Jim's car. Jim waved to the security guard when the barrier was lifted to allow us to pass, and came to a stop before turning right onto the highway. He looked both ways to ensure the road was clear before proceeding.

"You have to drive very defensively over here," Jim said. "You'll find that there are some of the worst drivers in the world in Saudi. They don't seem to have any respect for the rules of the road, or human life, and do the most stupid things at times. Most of them don't obey the speed limits either, so be very careful."

Traffic was light at six fifteen in the morning, but picked up as we got closer to Dhahran. I was full of questions as we made our way to work.

"What's that complex on the left?"

"That's the United States Military base" Jim advised.

"What's that structure on the hill?" I asked.

"That's the University of Dhahran," replied Jim, and so it went on as my curiosity ran rampant.

The darkness was quickly giving way to the grey light of dawn as we made our way past a shantytown on the sandy hillside just outside of Dhahran. The makeshift homes were made of cardboard and tin sheets, plastic sheeting and bits of lumber, anything that would serve to make an enclosure for habitation. I had seen similar shantytowns in Tijuana, Mexico, but didn't expect to see this in Saudi Arabia. Many of the small structures had a Datsun pick-up truck or small car parked alongside. Goats and chickens could be seen wandering around looking for food. Some of the shacks even had a television aerial projecting from the roof.

"Why is this shantytown here, just outside the camp gate?" I asked.

"Many of these people work for Aramco as gardeners or labourers," Jim said, "and living here they don't have far to go to work."

As we approached the main gate of Dhahran, a uniformed security guard signalled us to stop and approached Jim's vehicle. He could see the vehicle was an Aramco vehicle by the identification number stencilled on the side. He wrote down the number, and then asked Jim his destination. Jim replied "Dhahran Heights," and the guard waved him through.

Dhahran is not a town, as is believed by many people who've never visited Saudi Arabia. It is the first Aramco compound that was developed in Saudi Arabia when oil was first discovered in 1934. It was named after Jebel Dhahran where Aramco first struck oil. A plaque now marks the spot where the black gold first shot out of the ground. Dhahran grew from a small storage area with worker housing to a gated and fenced compound that today is the heart of Aramco's engineering and exploration divisions. It is also a residential compound that houses approximately 30,000 Aramco employees of various nationalities (including Saudis). It is the central hub for everything that Aramco does in Saudi Arabia.

As we drove through the tarmacked streets of the main office and storage areas at 6:50 a.m., people were arriving for work by bicycle, on foot, in private cars and Aramco vehicles. Some of the buildings are stone or brick built, whilst others are temporary trailer-type buildings prefabricated by ATCO in Canada.

We passed by several large steel buildings. Jim said they were maintenance workshops and equipment storage for Aramco's numerous endeavours relating to oil facilities and infrastructure development in the kingdom.

We arrived at a long, white ATCO portable building that stood alone on a rise near the compound's perimeter fence. Jim parked in the parking lot adjacent to the building.

"This is the offices of the Vendor Inspection Division (VID), and the Projects Inspection Division (PID)," Jim advised me.

The portable building had a hallway running down the centre with offices on either side.

"The far half of this building is the Projects Inspection Division," Jim said, "and VID is in this first half."

The offices weren't anything fancy, a typical construction site portable building. Steel desks with green Formica tops and steel filing cabinets seem to be standard, I noticed. We made our way down the hallway to the inspection supervisor's office.

"This is Dave Hansen," Jim said, as he introduced me to my supervisor.

After a brief chat, Dave advised me that I would be taking a safety course, a first aid course and an orientation class starting tomorrow. The courses and orientation would last for three days. He said there was no need to come to the office before the programs started.

"Show Mark around and introduce him to the other inspectors," Dave said to Jim, "and I'll catch up with him later. And Jim, take him to the passport office to deposit his passports, please. You have your passports with you, Mark?"

"Sure do," I said.

Jim took me to my new office.

"You'll be sharing an office with me and Floyd Harper," Jim said. "He should be here soon unless he has gone straight to a job site."

The office was sparsely furnished with three steel desks with green Formica tops and steel filing cabinets similar to the other offices I had observed.

"This will be your desk," Jim said. "Make a list of office supplies that you need if they aren't already in the desk, and I'll give the list to the secretary for him to requisition."

Whilst I was going through the desk checking to see what stationery and office equipment I needed, Dave Hansen came in and gave me a form to complete.

"You'll find this form self-explanatory. We'll circulate it around the office as kind of an introduction to the other people in the department. They'll then know your past experience and qualifications, should they need help in your area of expertise. It just needs to be a brief outline, so don't go into a lot of detail. Please give it to the secretary for typing when you've completed it. Then return it to me please."

"The secretary's name is Chandra," Jim advised. "He is in the end office. He is from India, and has been with us for several months. He makes a few typos so make sure you proofread his work."

When I had completed the form, I took it to Chandra and introduced myself.

"Where are you from?" he asked.

"Calgary, Alberta, Canada," I replied.

"It's cold there isn't it?"

"Sometimes."

Strange how everyone thinks of the cold when you mention Canada, I thought.

"Where are you from Chandra?"

"New Delhi," he replied.

"Do you have a family there?" I asked.

"Yes, my wife and three children are there. I go back to see them once a year. I'm due to go back in three months' time. I'm really looking forward to seeing them again."

When I returned to my office, Jim introduced me to Floyd Harper, who'd just arrived from a brief field trip. Floyd was tall and slim, had black curly hair and a moustache.

"Hi Mark, how was your trip over, boy'o?" he asked.

I recognized the unmistakable accent right away, Floyd was from Wales! Floyd is one of those people who you like immediately. It was easy to make a conversation with him, and he seemed very polite and congenial. I was glad that I was sharing an office with him, and knew that we would get along well.

Jim took me to the other VID offices and introduced me to the inspectors. First there was Gerry Morrow. He was a tall well-built man with a pockmarked face and a deadpan expression. First impression was that he didn't seem very friendly, but perhaps I was wrong about that. Jim later told me that Gerry was once a lay preacher, and then later a Texas Highway Patrol officer. I wondered how he became involved with quality assurance in the oil industry, after having those two unrelated jobs.

Next was Lorne Isborne. He was tall, overweight and balding, and wore glasses. About age 58, I guessed. He seemed to be a warm, friendly and easygoing man, and had a firm grip when he shook my hand. (I would later share an office with Lorne and Floyd when the department moved into a new building).

Austin Barton was next. He was medium height, black hair and greying beard, and partly balding. He had an American accent having spent most of his life in the United States. I later learned that he may be Jewish. (Austin wouldn't have been able to acknowledge that while living in the kingdom). He sported a gold Rolex watch on his left wrist, studded with diamonds. On his right wrist he had a heavy gold identity bracelet, and wore a heavy gold chain around his neck. Many expatriate workers, or expats as they were referred to, took the opportunity to buy 18-carat gold jewellery and watches. Gold products could be purchased at a very reasonable price in Saudi Arabia. For a 25-year-long service award, Aramco gave its employees a gold Rolex watch with a gold band. These watches were valued at about 8,000 United States dollars. Quite often a Saudi employee, who received a watch, would sell it by placing a notice on a company notice board. Five to six thousand dollars seemed to be the typical asking price. Many expats would snap up these watches. (Austin obviously liked material things, and liked to flaunt his wealth.) Austin shared an office with Daren Leman.

Daren Leman was a tall soft-spoken Texan in his early forties with a ruddy complexion and a beard. He was a little overweight with a belly that hung over his belt, but wasn't fat in other ways. Daren was one of the nicer Americans, not pretentious and never bragged unless it was about the size of the fish he caught. Then, like many anglers, he tended to exaggerate.

Steve Carmichael also shared an office with Austin and Daren. He was from the Lake District of England and had a northern accent. Baby-face came to mind when I was introduced to him. I estimated that he was in his mid-thirties. He was about five foot ten and had a stocky build.

Coming from northern England he probably liked his beer as many northerners do, I thought.

Robin Parker, an Englishman from Croydon, was in the end office and was the last inspector to be introduced. Robin was a wiry man about five foot eight with sandy hair that was starting to thin on top. He greeted me with a gentle handshake and wished me well in my new position. He was soft spoken and gave the impression of being easy going and congenial. He was on single status in Dhahran, as were most of the Brits, and shared a small condo apartment with Steve Carmichael.

"I think you've met everyone now," Jim said, "except for Dennis McBride, a young Scotsman who's on repatriation leave (referred to as repat) at the moment. He is a servorg," Jim said, "and will be back in Saudi in about two weeks. He shares an office with Robin."

"What's a servorg?" I inquired.

"That's an abbreviation we use for service organization. Aramco has lots of personnel who're hired through a service organization rather than direct hire such as you and me. The advantage of hiring a servorg is that Aramco can lay them off at short notice. Also they don't get many of the benefits, privileges and training that direct hires do. For instance, they can't use the library, cinema, bowling alley or swimming pool on camp. The organization that hires them is responsible for their accommodation off camp. Generally it is in a compound in Dammam or Al-Khobar, which would have very limited leisure facilities."

"Let's get a cup of coffee," Jim said. "Then I'll show you around Dhahran and we'll swing by the passport office so that you can turn in your passports."

The VID trailer offices were air conditioned with window-type air conditioners that were quite noisy.

"You'll get used to that racket," Jim said. "After a while you won't notice it. It's better than having no AC like some of our vehicles."

"Are you telling me that company vehicles aren't air conditioned," I exclaimed.

"Some of our trucks aren't. When Aramco ordered the last fleet of vehicles, many of the trucks arrived without AC by mistake. Fortunately they're now about two years old and are due for changing. The new ones will all have AC. If you're going on a long trip such as to Ras Tanura or Abqaiq, you make sure you take a department vehicle that has AC. Otherwise you'll cook! The department tries to use the vehicles with no AC for short trips in and around camp. You can always go to the car pool and get a vehicle if all the air-conditioned vehicles are being used."

I questioned why Aramco would buy vehicles with no AC.

Vehicles with no AC- something else they didn't tell us at orientation, I thought.

Jim said that they were ordered with AC, but when they arrived in Arabia a number of both the cars and trucks didn't have AC, and it wasn't cost effective to return them.

The car that Jim and I came to work in was assigned to Dave Hansen, the department supervisor. Jim had borrowed it from Dave so that he could pick up Monica, Blaine and me from the airport. Jim had a pick-up truck assigned to him so that he could get back and forth from Sea View rather than take the bus.

"You can ride with me in the morning and evenings," Jim said. "No point in taking the bus if you don't need to."

Jim's truck didn't have AC I noticed, as Jim took me on a tour of Dhahran. In January the daytime temperature is comfortable—a light windbreaker is sometimes needed. Jim pointed out the commissary where basic grocery provisions could be purchased, as well as small hardware items. Next to the commissary was the mail centre. Jim stopped the truck to go in and check his mailbox. Next to the mail centre was a hairdressing salon.

"The hairdresser is Lebanese," Jim said. "You have to make an appointment if you need a cut, and we generally do it on company time. The salon is only open during working hours during the week, and on Thursday mornings." (The weekend in Saudi Arabia is Thursday and Friday—equivalent to Saturday and Sunday in the Western world). "He is not the greatest barber, but the cost is reasonable and it is better than trying to find a barber off camp."

The next stop was the library. It reminded me of the typical small town library back home. It was stocked with a good selection of popular North American magazines and periodicals, as well as newspapers from many of the large American and Canadian cities. Comfortable lounge chairs were in abundance. At ten thirty in the morning there were a surprising number of people making use of the services it provided.

"The magazines are all checked for pictures that wouldn't be considered suitable for the Middle Eastern culture," Jim remarked. "Pictures of women in underwear and bathing suits are blacked out with a felt pen, and any reference to Israel is also blacked out."

Jim pointed out the bowling alley, and then we made a stop at the swimming pool. The pool was covered with a sunroof to prevent the water from becoming too hot. Jim said that they have a chiller in the water circulation system, as the water would get far too uncomfortable in the summer months without it. Lounge chairs were plentiful, and Jim and I made use of two of them to relax for a while. Although it was wintertime, there were several people in the pool doing laps in the roped off lanes, and a mother with her two young children were splashing around in the shallow end.

"Life is sure tough in the desert," Jim remarked, as he lay back enjoying the warm rays of the sun. "Aramco brings in American swimming instructors from time to time to teach the kids swimming and diving. You may want to make use of that for Blaine," Jim said. "They also run adult swimming and exercise classes for all level of expertise, and it is free to Aramcons."

"I'll take you to the area they call Dhahran Hills," Jim said, as we got back into Jim's truck to complete our tour of Dhahran.

"The Hills is a new housing area that's still under construction. It will provide permanent housing to a lot of Aramco personnel when completed. About a hundred homes have been completed to date and are now occupied."

The streets of Dhahran in the residential areas are paved, and have sidewalks similar to any American or Canadian city. The area of permanent homes reminded me of a typical California suburb. Lawns were neatly manicured, and palm trees, shrubs and flowers were in abundance. Many of the homes were large bungalows faced with brick and stone, similar to western architecture. Some had stucco walls with arched entrances and wrought-iron gates. At the end of the older part of the Dhahran residential area was a block of adobe-style homes. They were for the single Aramcons, most of whom were British. Aramco didn't provide family status for the Brits.

As the sidewalks ended, the road dipped down through the sand dunes.

"To the left is the Aramco Golf Course," Jim said. "The greens are black because they're oiled surfaces to prevent the sand from blowing away, and it provides a smooth surface for putting. I bet you've never seen anything like that before."

Opposite the golf course was a helicopter pad, which I would later use to fly offshore to an Aramco barge.

We had a good view of Dhahran Hills from this elevated location. It looked quite different from the older part of Dhahran that we'd just driven through. Dhahran Hills is a housing complex surrounded by the desert. It had no trees or vegetation except for sparsely planted grass outside some of the completed homes. The roads were paved and had sidewalks, and street lighting was installed.

Some of the homes appeared similar to the typical home back in Canada, I thought.

Others were adobe-style flat roofed two-storey structures with a brown stucco finish, and an eight-foot stucco wall around the perimeter. (Monica and I were later housed in one of these homes when we received our permanent housing). We drove around for about twenty minutes as Jim gave me a tour of the completed homes, as well as those under construction.

"They're currently building about three to four hundred homes in the Hills," Jim said, "as well as a school and a swimming pool. They have buses that run from the Hills to the offices and Aramco facilities, for employees and their families who don't have a car. It is about a fifteen-minute drive to our office from here," Jim said.

As it was nearly midday, Jim suggested that we go to the Aramco cafeteria for lunch. The cafeteria was starting to fill up with people from the Aramco offices, but the self-service lineup wasn't too long.

"If you want a hot lunch they have a choice of three or four dishes to choose from, or you can get a sandwich or pastry if you only want a light snack," Jim said.

We both chose a sandwich and coffee and made our way to a table near the window.

That was a wide selection of food, I thought.

The service was quick and well organized, and the cost was reasonable.

A good place to have lunch, I'll be coming here often, I thought.

After lunch, Jim continued his tour of the camp. He showed me the movie theatre, ball diamonds, children's playground, bank, the Dhahran Hospital and the Aramco guest house. The guest house was a large stone-faced bungalow surrounded with palm trees, shrubs and neatly manicured lawns.

"The dignitaries stay there when they come to Dhahran," Jim said. "I didn't get an invite; I can't understand why," he joked.

We drove over to the passport office and I handed over our passports to the Saudi at the desk. He was dressed in a white Thobe and red check Gutra, which is typical attire for many of the Saudi employees.

"When you leave the kingdom, you have to give the Passport Office two to three weeks notice so that they can get an Exit and Re-entry permit put in your passports. Otherwise you'll not be allowed to leave the kingdom," Jim advised.

We returned to the office at Dhahran Heights, and I found the completed form that I had given to Chandra on my desk. I gave it a quick proofread and found no mistakes, so I dropped it in Dave Hansen's in-tray. Later that afternoon Dave came to see me and advised me that the Vendor Inspection Division rarely had any work involving instrumentation or electrical equipment. But should the opportunity arise, he would make sure that I would be assigned.

This came as a complete shock to me. I wondered why Aramco would have hired someone with extensive experience with electrical equipment and instrumentation, and put them in a position where this experience couldn't be utilized. I also had experience with the inspection of mechanical equipment such as pumps, compressors, valves and pressure vessels, but this wasn't my area of expertise.

Jim could see that I was concerned about this revelation and said "Don't worry about it, Mark, we'll find something to keep you busy. Aramco will train you if they feel you're lacking knowledge in a specific field you're working in."

Jim advised me that everyone in the office was expected to train young Saudi employees during the summer months.

"Aramco sends them to university in the United States during the winter. They return to Saudi Arabia for work experience with Aramco when university is out. We generally get two or three in our office for training, and they can all speak reasonable English. Most of them are interested in learning all they can, so that helps."

It was nearing 4:00 p.m., so Jim and I had a quick cup of coffee and left for home in Jim's truck. We stopped off at the commissary so that Jim could pick up a few provisions before leaving Dhahran. I was able to get an idea of the grocery items that Aramco stocked, and found most of the basic canned, boxed and packaged foods were available. However, there weren't a variety of brands.

"Pork is not available in Saudi Arabia, as it is against the Islamic religion to eat pork," Jim said. "However, Aramco has a pork store in the commissary where expats can buy bacon, pork roasts, chops and sausages. You have to show your Aramco ID (identification card), and you're limited to a specific quantity each month."

On the drive back to Sea View, I had many questions for Jim about Dhahran and life in Saudi Arabia. Jim had been in Saudi Arabia for about six months. He was familiar with the local towns of Al-Khobar and Dammam, and had visited some of the Aramco gas plants and refineries.

"You'll notice that there are no directional signs or mileage signs for the local towns," Jim said. "You have to learn to find your way around in the local communities. You may want to pay attention to the route we take to and from work, so that when you get your driving licence you'll not get lost. The first few times you go to the local town and Aramco plants, you'll be with someone from the office who'll show you where to go. Al-Khobar is reasonably easy to find your way around, but Dammam can be confusing the first few times you go there."

Jim gave me the impression that he and Annette were reasonably happy in Saudi Arabia, but would be glad when they received their temporary house on camp. Then they wouldn't have the drive to Sea View each day, and would be able to use some of the on-camp facilities in the evenings. Jim advised me that Aramco vehicles are for work use only, and could be used for driving to and from work. They can't be used for personal use without prior approval.

When I arrived home, Monica was busy preparing the evening meal. She and Blaine had toured Sea View and met a few of the neighbours. They'd spent some time with Linda Griffin and her two children, Lorna and Annette. (Monica had met Linda and her husband, Ted, in the fall before they left Canada). Linda and Monica had arranged to meet the following day and were going to take the Aramco bus to Dhahran to get some groceries. Monica also met a lady called Jamie Baynes, who had a three-year-old girl named Shane. Her husband worked in non-destructive testing for Aramco.

CHAPTER 6

Safety First

After my first day, I spent the next three days taking a safety course, a first aid course and an orientation class about life in Saudi Arabia. Jim dropped me off at the classroom in the morning, and picked me up at four o'clock each day.

Safety is a top priority for Aramco, and it was covered in detail in the first class I attended. There were about thirty new hires in the class from various Aramco camps and departments. Driving in Saudi Arabia was the first item on the agenda, and it was made clear that after three accidents you're sent home. We were advised most motor vehicle accidents are avoidable. Numerous real life examples were reviewed and the class was asked to judge if they were preventable or non-preventable. In some cases, the people who were involved in an accident were brought in to talk to the class. They talked about their experience, and the repercussions on their work and family life. One engineer, who I would meet again during the course of my work, nearly lost his life due to serious head and leg injuries. As a result, he now walked with a limp and the assistance of a cane.

The class was advised that from May to July there are often strong winds in Saudi Arabia called 'shamals'. A shamal is a violent and dusty wind from the north that stirs up sandstorms. It picks up the desert sand and can make driving visibility very bad—similar to a snow blizzard. A shamal can last from a few hours to several days. It is advised never to drive if a shamal is blowing. Visibility can suddenly go to zero, and you can find yourself stranded in the hot desert heat.

"Always take a water igloo with you when you go on a trip in case you break down. Never leave your vehicle as it can provide shade. If you're overdue from a trip and a search party is sent out to look for you, they'll be looking for your vehicle. So never wander into the desert away from your vehicle," the instructor impressed upon us.

The instructor related a story about two pipeline workers who wandered away from their vehicle and got lost in the desert. When they found their bodies, they were burnt black from the desert sun.

An overview of hydrogen sulphide poisoning was given. All employees have to take the Aramco H2S Alive program that their supervisor arranges.

Also, employees who travel off camp will be required to pick up a water igloo, safety footwear and safety glasses from the Aramco safety supply department. New safety footwear will be issued every six months if needed.

All new hires were put through a practical driving test in an Aramco truck. I was asked to narrate my actions and thoughts as I drove the test vehicle, which

I found unusual. I passed without any comments. The instructor impressed the need to drive defensively, as there are a lot of exceptionally bad Saudi drivers around. There are repercussions such as arrest and imprisonment even if it is not your fault. Usually, the Saudi police put everyone in jail whilst they sort things out if you're not injured. Typically, at least fifty percent of the blame is assigned to expatriate workers, whether it is their fault or not.

The following day we were given a first aid manual, and received instruction on basic first aid. It was similar to the first aid classes I had attended back home. I found it good to have a refresher as there were some things I had forgotten over the years. This class also covered an in-depth review of heatstroke and how to treat it in an emergency.

During my lunch break, I met one of the chemical engineers I had first met in Houston. He told me that he was stationed in Abqaiq, an Aramco community and refinery about ninety minutes' drive south west of Dhahran. He was very dissatisfied with his new job, as Aramco had put him in a position as a mechanical engineer at the refinery. He said he wasn't familiar with pumps, valves and compressors and the like, and thought he might decide to go home. I told him that I specialized in the inspection of electrical equipment and instrumentation. The department where I had been assigned had little in the way of this kind of work.

"I can understand your concerns. Hang in there," I told him. "See how it works out. Don't make a quick decision that you may regret later."

On the third day we went through an orientation program that covered many aspects of living and working in Saudi Arabia.

- How to dress for both the employee and the family.
- What to do at prayer break if you're shopping.
- Do's and don'ts in the local communities, and how to treat the Saudis with respect and dignity.
- What happens if you're arrested for a driving infraction or an accident.
- Training of Saudi employees.
- What to do if you get lost.
- Language classes in Arabic, which Aramco offers.
- Giving blood at the blood donor clinic.
- Use of Aramco recreational facilities.
- Use of Aramco bus system.
- Travelling to other Aramco camps and facilities.
- How to buy a car and how to get a driver's licence.

There were many good pointers and tips that I made a note of to relay to Monica when I returned home.

CHAPTER 7

Ju'aymah and Ras Tanura

When Jim and I were driving to work on Wednesday morning, Jim said he had to go to the Ju'aymah gas plant that morning to meet one of its engineers. He had to discuss a valve problem that the plant was having and look at some defective valves. Jim arranged for me to go with him so that I would know how to get to the Ju'aymah plant in future. We checked in at the office for a quick cup of coffee before leaving. I was given a voucher for safety boots and a hard hat, which Jim said I had to get before we departed.

"If you don't have safety boots and a hard hat, they'll not let you into the plant."

After I had picked up my safety equipment, we departed for Ju'aymah. Jim filled up his truck at the Aramco gas station. We exited the north gate of Dhahran for our trip to the gas plant.

About five kilometres past the North gate, a railroad track crosses the two-lane highway. Just as we approached the tracks a freight train started to cross the road blocking the highway. The train was moving very slowly so Jim came to a stop and turned off the ignition. He anticipated a long wait. Cars and trucks started to back up behind us. To my amazement another line of traffic quickly formed on the opposite side of the road in the oncoming lane. More traffic formed lines in the flat sandy desert on either side of the two lane highway, creating several more lines of cars heading north. As the freight cars passed, I could see that traffic had also built up on the opposite side of the track in a similar pattern. I thought this would lead to a real problem when the freight train cleared the track.

"This should be interesting," I commented.

"Yes it will be, but it will all sort itself out as you'll see," Jim replied.

When the freight train eventually passed, there was a mad shuffling of traffic, with horns blowing and arms waving. Frustrated drivers tried to thread their way through the mess of vehicles going in all directions, in an effort to get back onto the highway on the correct side of the road.

I remembered that I had been told about this at my orientation in Houston, but didn't expect to see it for myself. This must happen all the time, I realised.

Another experience that will live in my memory, I thought.

The road to Ju'aymah and Ras Tanura is a two-lane, blacktop highway. It winds through the desert sand dunes, with many hills and valleys and gentle curves as it heads northward. During our trip, Jim had to drive off the road and into the desert several times to avoid oncoming vehicles that were overtaking on the brow of a hill or on a curve in the road.

"This is a normal part of driving in the kingdom," he remarked. "You have to drive with your wits about you all the time and expect anything. They impress on you to drive defensively and they really mean it. They tell me that people in the medical vehicles that are called out to attend a traffic accident have very little training. They basically bundle you into the emergency vehicle and get you to the nearest hospital."

I wondered if we would make it to the Ju'aymah gas plant without an accident! I was very concerned for my safety. During the trip I noticed a number of smashed-up and burnt-out vehicles in the desert beside the highway. I couldn't help wondering how many people had succumbed to a horrific death, or been scarred for life in fiery crashes in the sweltering heat of the desert a long way from medical attention. It was a chilling thought, and it unnerved me a little as I thought of the reality of an accident so far from home and medical attention.

The road to Ju'aymah is broken up in places and has numerous potholes that can test the springs on most vehicles. After travelling for about forty-five minutes, we stopped off at a little village to get a cold drink. To say that it was a total mess wouldn't be an exaggeration. Potholes in the road were deep in this little village, perhaps left that way intentionally, I wondered, to slow the traffic down. Chickens, dogs and goats seem to wander at will, looking for morsels of food. Most of the buildings were ramshackle and in need of repair. Junk and garbage appeared to be left wherever it was dropped on the sandy sidewalks or beside the buildings.

Jim stopped the truck outside a small store selling soft drinks and got us both an ice cold Pepsi. As we were drinking our Pepsi, Jim told me a story about an engineer from Ras Tanura who went to the Dhahran airport to pick up a new hire from Houston. As they entered this little village on their way back to Ras Tanura, the engineer turned to the new hire and said, "Well here we are; this is the Aramco camp!" By all accounts the new hire was prepared to turn around and go home immediately.

For some reason, the Saudi Military has a small base in this little village, and the buildings they were housed in appeared to be in no better shape than the village.

When we arrived at the Ju'aymah gas plant, Jim stopped at the security gate and signed in with the date and time of arrival. The security guard checked our Aramco ID cards and waved us through. The engineering department was housed in portable-type buildings, similar to those of our own department in Dhahran. Jim met with one of the plant engineers to review the problem they were having with their control valves. He reviewed quality measures to be put in place to prevent future occurrence.

It was lunchtime when business was concluded, so we decided to stop for lunch at the plant cafeteria. Jim had two lunch tickets that he was given for the trip, so it was a free meal for us both. Jim said that each year the cafeterias at the gas plants and refineries compete for the best food. The Shedgum gas plant nearly always wins it with a really outstanding selection of food.

After lunch we signed out at the security gate. Jim said he would take me on a tour of the Ras Tanura camp, which was about twenty minutes' drive from Ju'aymah.

"The Ras Tanura camp is smaller than the Dhahran camp," Jim said, "but it is a desirable place to live for many people because some of the houses back onto the beach. All the houses are within walking distance of the beach."

Najmah compound (Aramco code: RT) is one of four residential compounds built by Aramco in the 1940s and the only one located on the Gulf itself. A heavily guarded security fence surrounds Ras Tanura refinery. Saudi employees and their dependants may live inside the Najmah residential compound, which is less heavily guarded. It was originally built to allow expatriate oil company employees (mainly Americans) a degree of western comfort and separation from the restrictions of Saudi and Islamic laws.

After signing in at the Ras Tanura (Najmah) security gate, we passed through another security gate to tour the refinery. A vehicle is needed to drive around the refinery, as it is massive in proportion to anything I had ever seen before. A conglomeration of piping, towers, pressure vessels and stacks covered many acres that produce 265,000 barrels of oil per day. It is shipped by super tanker around the world.

"As long as you don't mind a 90-minute drive to get to the Dhahran airport, and a 60-minute drive to Dammam for shopping, the Najmah compound is a great place to live," Jim said.

After our tour of the refinery and Najmah compound, we headed back to Dhahran. It was 3:30 p.m. by the time we got back to our office in Dhahran. Just enough time for a quick cup of coffee before the drive back to Sea View, and the end of my first week in the kingdom.

THE FIRST THREE MONTHS 51

CHAPTER 8

The First Three Months

It was good to sleep in on Thursday morning, first day of the weekend. After a lazy breakfast and a shower, Monica and I decided to catch the bus into Dhahran and take Blaine for a swim in the pool. The Sea View pool didn't have any water in it for some reason, and wouldn't have any water for as long as we lived there.

It would be Monica's second trip to Dhahran. She'd visited the camp on the previous Saturday with the wives of other new arrivals to get her Aramco ID card, and to attend a new arrivals orientation. The Aramco Greyhound bus arrived at Sea View at eleven-o-clock, and about a dozen people boarded for the trip to Dhahran. Before going to Dhahran, the bus made a detour to the Al-Gasabi apartment block, another Aramco housing complex in the suburbs of Al-Khobar, to pick up more people. Garth and Danielle Fenton and their two sons, Garth Junior and James, boarded the bus, and recognised Monica and me from the orientation in Houston. They sat in front of us and were glad to see someone they knew. Danielle said that she hadn't been out of their apartment all week as Garth had told her that women had to be accompanied by their husbands to go out in public. She'd spent a quiet week with the two boys with very little to do, and no friends in their building. She was glad that the weekend had arrived as she was tired of being cooped up in their small apartment.

It had rained overnight as was evident by the large puddles of water in some of the streets of Al Khobar and on the highway to Dhahran. The bus occasionally splashed through the pooled water that was lying in the roadway in a number of areas. There is no drainage in Saudi Arabia. Any rainwater collects in the low-lying areas and forms large pools of water that sometimes floods some of the buildings. Fortunately, they don't get a lot of precipitation for most of the year. January and February can be a little wet some years, as was the case this year.

The bus dropped us off at the commissary. With a small map of Dhahran that Aramco provided with an information package in our condo, we found our way to the swimming pool. We showed our Aramco passes to a security guard at the pool entrance. Blaine was about five months old at this point and couldn't swim. He really enjoyed his first dip in the pool with his little water wings for flotation. He didn't seem to have any fear of the water and took to it like a duck. He didn't want to get out. After our swim, we relaxed on lounge chairs enjoying the warmth of the sun, although there was a winter chill in the air.

I took Monica and Blaine to the library where they read children's books, magazines and periodicals until Blaine became impatient and wanted to get on the move. The snack bar was close at hand so we got a burger and fries. Blaine was tired after his swim, and went to sleep in his pushchair. We had about an hour to wait before the Greyhound bus departed for Sea View. We walked over to the post office and commissary, so that Monica could become familiar with these two facilities for future visits to Dhahran. We passed the Aramco dining hall on the way.

When we boarded the bus for our return trip, Garth and Danielle Fenton and their two sons were already on board. They'd boarded at the snack bar bus stop. It had started to rain again, which we didn't expect to see in this land of eternal sunshine. Danielle and Monica arranged to meet during the week for a bus trip to the Al Khobar Safeway store. Danielle had heard about Safeway but hadn't been there yet.

On Sunday, Monica boarded the Greyhound bus in Sea View for her trip to the Safeway store. Danielle and her younger son James had come over from the Al-Gasabi apartment. The bus only went directly from Sea View to the Safeway store and back again. The bus driver, a Philippine national, helped Monica on the bus with her pushchair. There were no other passengers besides her and Danielle when the bus departed for Safeway. The Safeway store was similar to the Safeway stores in North America except all the pricing was in Saudi riyals. Most of the attendants in the store were from India, Pakistan or the Philippines, and all were men.

Monica had been to Safeway before, when we stopped briefly on our way to Sea View when we first arrived. She could remember little about it as she was so tired from our long trip from Houston.

Very few women are found in service jobs in Saudi Arabia, the exception being for office jobs within Aramco. Except for the Saudi men in their thobes and gutras, sometimes accompanied by their wife in a black abaya, Danielle and Monica felt like they were back home shopping. They loaded their baskets with groceries and headed for the checkout. The Greyhound bus was waiting in the parking lot with its engine running to keep the bus cool inside. The bus driver helped them on the bus with their groceries, and they departed for home.

"That's what you call service," Monica remarked. "Our own bus to go shopping. You don't get that back home."

* * * * *

As Aramco projects were completed throughout Saudi Arabia, there would quite often be surplus materials due to design changes, equipment amendments or over supply. These surplus materials were consolidated in a yard on the outskirts of Dhahran. Dave Hansen asked Jim DeAngelo and me to visit the Surplus Yard to conduct an assessment of storage procedures. Also to find out what class of materials were stored in this yard. He indicated that at the present time new project groups weren't adequately utilizing surplus materials. As a result, some of the materials in the yard were suffering degradation due to long-term and inadequate storage. He indicated that the Vendor Inspection Division had been asked to inspect the materials in the yard for condition and future project use. Also, to determine if storage conditions and cataloguing needed to be improved or amended.

When Jim and I arrived at the Surplus Yard in Jim's pickup truck, a security guard stopped us at the barrier and asked for our identification. Jim signed in and parked his truck at the portable office building at the yard entrance. We went inside to talk to the yard manager. Jim explained the purpose of our visit. The yard manager was a tall bald-headed Texan who looked like the New York City police detective from the TV series Kojak (Telly Savalas). He indicated that if we needed any assistance or office space for our work, he would be happy to assist and provide whatever we needed. He explained that his team of people who worked in the yard consisted of about fifteen Filipino and Indian nationals. They catalogued all the materials in the yard as best they could, and the catalogue was distributed to Aramco project groups throughout Saudi Arabia.

"We don't determine the condition of the materials," he said, "unless they're obviously no good and then they're sent to the reclamation yard. You'll need to drive around the yard as it is quite large."

Jim decided the first thing we needed to do was get an idea of the size of the yard, and materials that were in storage. As we departed the office complex in Jim's truck, we quickly realized the yard was vast—bigger than anything we'd imagined. After driving for about thirty minutes down the rows of surplus materials, Jim estimated it was about 100 acres in size. It contained all manner of materials from surplus pipe up to 56 inches in diameter, control valves, electrical conduit and fittings, control panels, electrical switch gear, breaker panels, pressure transmitters, pressure vessels, compressors and pumps. Almost anything that would be associated with plant construction. We couldn't believe the size of the yard, the amount of materials in storage, and the deplorable storage conditions. Most of the materials were dumped in the desert sand, sometimes on wooden pallets, and sometimes covered with a plastic sheeting for protection. I took a quick look at some of the electrical equipment. I realized that as a result of the sand that had blown inside some of the equipment, it wouldn't be worthwhile trying to save it. It should be scrapped.

"We've got a mammoth job here," Jim exclaimed. "A lot of this material is not adequately identified by the surplus yard. Much of it needs to be scrapped because of sand contamination, or degradation occurring due to poor storage. Where do we start?"

On our way back to the office, we decided this job could take several years to complete due to the volume and diversity of equipment in the Surplus Yard. Technical expertise was needed to describe and catalogue the equipment as well as procedures required to inspect it. Once in place, a catalogue of procedures would also help inspectors and Saudi nationals with future projects. We would also need office space in the office building in the Surplus Yard. Several written recommendations were made to Dave Hansen following our return to Dhahran Heights. They were subsequently accepted, and we were given the go ahead to proceed and to report our progress on a monthly basis.

This wasn't the job I had anticipated doing when I came to Arabia. But, as Jim said, "Why complain, it is not forever and we're being paid well."

I had to agree. Jim and I started to write procedures for inspection of materials. I was concentrating on the electrical and instrumentation, and Jim on mechanical equipment. Office desks were set up in the Surplus Yard office building so that travelling was minimized. We were warned to be aware of snakes and scorpions when handling equipment in the yard. However, only once did we come across a snake during our time in the yard. It quickly ran for cover when it was disturbed.

As March and April came around the temperature started to increase, and working outside necessitated frequent breaks to get out of the hot sun. May to July is the shamal season, bringing violent and dusty winds from the north. With the high temperatures and humidity, it is very uncomfortable to be outdoors. All exposed skin becomes caked in sand we soon found out, especially if you've been sweating. It also gets on your teeth and crunches in your mouth, and finds its way inside your clothing.

It was hot and tiring work. We often parked our pick-up truck close to the equipment we were inspecting, keeping the engine running to keep the cab cool whilst doing our visual examination. Then we would jump back in the truck again to cool off and drink some water. This work went on for several months, and it seemed like we were only just scratching the surface of the problem. Numerous pieces of plant equipment were scrapped. Because the degradation from exposure and bad storage was too excessive, restoration would be too costly. At times it seemed like a daunting task, but gradually we started making headway.

CHAPTER 9

Moon Base Charley

All expatriate workers must leave the kingdom for a minimum of 21 days each year. Aramco provides a full fare ticket for the employee and dependants to go back to the point of hire. The tickets are paid in cash to the employee. When Blaine was under two years old, he sat on my lap or Monica's during flights. However, he still received cash for the equivalent of a full fare ticket home.

When an employee goes on repatriation leave, someone in his department has to look after his work while he is away.

Most employees took one to three holidays a year. Quite often the holiday was booked through a group trip that was organized by an employee on camp. Many Aramcons ran small sideline businesses to make extra money. A travel business organizer would arrange trips to places such as Egypt, India, Greece or Cyprus. The person organizing the trip would go for free, or receive a kickback from the travel agent with whom they were associated. Other businesses included making artwork and selling it, or babysitting for mothers who wanted to work for Aramco. Making and selling illicit alcohol was another very profitable but highly illegal sideline.

Jim and I were sitting in the office one day when Austin Barton, who also shared the office at the time, said he was going to start a video club.

"When I go back on repat, I'm going to provide three friends with a new video recorder. I'll have them copy and send me three movies a week in return for the video recorder. I'll have the movies posted to me through a friend's post box on the United States forces base in Al-Khobar. The customs people won't have the chance to look at them because mail to the base is not examined. I'm sure they would confiscate them if women are seen in a bathing costume, or showing a bit of leg. You know what the Saudi authorities are like. I'll build up a tape club and rent the tapes out for $3 each for three days."

"Sounds like a good plan," Jim exclaimed.

When Austin returned from his repatriation vacation a month later he said he had it all organized.

"I'm getting nine new movies a week," he said. "Now I have a constant supply of new movies if you need something to watch."

Austin's movie club expanded to the point where he had hundreds of rental movies. He was making a nice profit from his club, all tax-free. During a meeting that I attended, Austin boasted that one day he would be so rich that he would be driving around Dhahran in a chauffeur-driven limousine. I told Jim about this, and he laughed and said, "I think Austin has visions of grandeur; perhaps the desert sun is getting to him."

Because of the shortage of housing, Aramco had set up a trailer camp called North Camp, just outside of Dhahran, where new employees could be housed. It consisted primarily of about a hundred and fifty ATCO trailer homes. They had been installed in rows in the desert, with tarmacked streets in between. They were hooked up to water, power, sewer and phone and street lighting was provided. In the middle of the camp there was a swimming pool, which was partly covered with a sunshade roof. As it was considered temporary housing, there were no trees, grass or shrubs. It was stark and bleak looking, especially when the sand was blowing in the shamal season. As a result, it got the nickname of Moon Base Charley. North Camp was about a ten-minute drive from Dhahran. Aramco provided a bus service into Dhahran at regular intervals during the day and evening. Many new employees who were offered housing here liked it for the convenience of being close to Dhahran. They could go into Dhahran for a movie or other entertainment in the evening, or to visit friends. Inside, the trailers were very comfortable and roomy and were equipped with well-appointed kitchens, two bedrooms and two bathrooms.

"We've been offered a trailer in North Camp," I told Monica one day.

Monica knew of the trailer camp but hadn't thought much about it until then. I had the key to the trailer we'd been offered, and after work I took Monica and Blaine on a tour of the camp and trailer. We both agreed that it would be much more convenient for Monica to visit Dhahran. Also a much shorter drive for me in the morning and evening to get to work and back.

"It will probably be another two years before we're offered temporary in-camp housing," I said. So we decided to accept the offer.

It didn't take long to move into North Camp as we had very few possessions. Clothing, kitchen utensils, Blaine's toys and push chair, and a few groceries was all we had. It was an easy move with a truck the department loaned me for the weekend. I was able to get the bus into work and back. After a few weeks, Austin Barton and his wife Lorna moved into the trailer nearby. Most mornings I would get a ride to work in Austin's car.

One Wednesday afternoon when I was leaving the office, Austin asked me if I would like a ride home.

"That would be great," I said.

"I have to go to the commissary before going back to North Camp," Austin said. "My wife is grocery shopping and I've arranged to pick her up. Is that okay?"

"Not a problem," I replied.

Austin was watching out for Lorna as we neared the commissary in Austin's car but didn't see her. I had never met Lorna so wouldn't be able to recognize her. Austin circled the commissary and parking lot several times looking for Lorna. As she was nowhere to be seen, Austin decided that she must still be finishing her grocery shopping. Austin parked for about ten minutes and then circled the commissary again. He spotted her near the Mail Centre standing beside the road with two carts of groceries. Austin parked next to her, and Austin and I got out and started to load the groceries into the car. Lorna was furious with Austin.

"I've been waiting for about fifteen to twenty minutes in the hot sun, and you drove by me three times and didn't stop. I was waving and shouting and still you didn't see me, you idiot!"

Lorna got into the car, and was still lacing into Austin while he and I were putting the groceries into the car. The berating she was giving Austin didn't let up! I was embarrassed as I packed the second cart of groceries into the trunk of Austin's car, and pretended not to hear Lorna's angry verbiage. I didn't have a good first impression of Lorna. During the drive back to North Camp, Lorna continued to chastise Austin, although she was starting to settle down.

"You've got a lot of groceries, Lorna," Austin remarked.

"Not that much Austin. You know we are having friends for supper tomorrow. I thought I would make sure I had everything I needed. Sometimes the commissary quickly runs out of some things like chocolate chips and some of the canned fruits. I have to take advantage of what's available whilst the stocks last."

"Of course my love," Austin replied in a calm voice, thankful that Lorna was finally settling down from her anger.

When I entered our trailer, Blaine came rushing to the door to greet me.

"Hey big boy what've you been doing today?" I asked, as I lifted him up for a hug.

"Swimming, Dad," he replied. "I swim fast."

"Blaine loves the water," Monica replied. "He is not afraid of it at all; he is doing really well."

"That's great," I replied.

Just after I sat down to supper, the telephone rang. "It's for you," Monica said just after she picked up the phone. "I think it is Austin."

"Hi Austin. Everything OK?"

I listened intently as Austin told me that a lot of the grocery items they were unpacking weren't items that Lorna had purchased.

"How can that be?" I asked.

"I can't imagine," said Austin. "Lorna said she definitely didn't buy a lot of these groceries."

There was a long silence and then I said, "You and I packed the groceries she had with her into the car. That's all I know. I don't know what else to say."

Austin said he would give me a ride to work in the morning, and said not to worry. He would get it sorted out.

When I told Monica what Austin had said, she was as baffled as I was.

"Perhaps she had a memory lapse," Monica said.

On the way into work in the morning, Austin said that Lorna still insisted she didn't buy some of the groceries.

"I can't figure out what she could have done," Austin said.

Austin, Jim and I were now sharing an office together. Over our first morning coffee, Austin told Jim the story about the groceries.

"Perhaps we should all come over to your trailer and help you eat them groceries," Jim joked.

Jim's wife Annette phoned, and Jim told her about the mysterious extra groceries.

"I told Austin we're coming over for supper," Jim said. "We got to help out a friend in need, don't you think."

Jim's wife worked at the Dhahran hospital in the administration department. It was a part-time job for five hours a day on weekdays. She liked to keep busy, and it paid well and provided some extra tax-free cash for travelling.

Jim and I were just about to leave the office to go to our other office in the Surplus Yard when Jim's phone rang.

"Hi Annette," Jim said. "You caught me as we were just about to leave." Jim listened intently and gave a chuckle. "I'll tell him. I guess that means we won't be invited around for supper. Bye for now."

Jim put the phone down and said to Austin, "You're in a pile of trouble friend. They cut your hand off for stealing in Saudi Arabia!"

"What do you mean?" Austin exclaimed.

"Annette just told me that there is a story going around the hospital about a Filipino houseboy. He went shopping for groceries yesterday afternoon for the people he works for. Apparently he left his grocery cart on the sidewalk whilst he got the car from the parking lot. By the time he got back to the shopping cart, someone had taken all his groceries."

"No shit!" said Austin.

"That's the story going around the hospital, Austin. You better get your butt over to see Annette. See if you can find out how to contact that houseboy or the people he works for. It seems obvious to me that you've got his groceries."

"Don't you laugh, Mark," Austin said. "They'll cut your hand off as well. You loaded them groceries into the car so you're just as guilty as I am."

Austin made a hasty retreat out of the office and headed for the hospital to see Annette.

"Come on Mark," Jim said. "Let's get down to the Surplus Yard before you get thrown in jail," he joked. "We've got a meeting to attend."

Later that afternoon when Jim and I returned to the office, we found Austin on the phone apologizing to someone for the mix-up with the groceries.

"I got damn all done today," Austin said after he got off the phone. "I found out whose groceries I have. I made a trip to North Camp to pick up the groceries from my trailer, and took them over to the people's house. They were really good about it as they realized it was an honest mistake. They said their houseboy was really upset and offered to pay for the groceries. Those houseboys don't make much money; it would be like a month's wages to him I'm sure."

"Sorry for all the trouble, Austin," I said. "I really thought that both carts of groceries were Lorna's."

"Well I did too," Austin said. "If Lorna hadn't been so uptight about having to wait a few minutes, this probably wouldn't have happened. Ah well, it's all taken care of now, let's forget about it."

Dhahran is the largest of the Aramco camps with about forty thousand people living within the fence. It's small compared to a North American town. Dhahran has its own radio station, but there is no newspaper. As a result, news is spread by word of mouth. The rumour mill is very active and news spreads like wildfire. As with all rumours, they get embellished as they spread. You're never quite sure how much truth there is to the story. However, most stories that circulate are basically true.

After I had been working at the Surplus Yard for about six months, I was transferred to the Purchasing department. The Vendor Inspection Division had just set up a small department to review all of Aramco's purchase orders. Purchase orders were written by engineers and purchasing agents at the Aramco camps throughout Arabia for materials and equipment for the various Aramco projects. All the purchase orders came into the Dhahran Purchasing Department for final preparation and issue. The Vendor Inspection Division found that many of the purchase orders didn't include adequate quality assurance and inspection data. This data was fundamental to ensure that a quality product was being shipped to Aramco. As a result, a three-man team of inspectors was assigned to the Dhahran Purchasing Department to review all purchase orders. It didn't matter how small the order or how large, or what its end use was, all purchase orders were reviewed by the Vendor Inspection Division.

Aramco has a continual turnover of personnel on the various projects due to attrition. As a result, training of new people is an ongoing process. Most of the purchase orders that I reviewed in the next few months were for engineered products such as electric motors, pumps, compressors, valves, pressure transmitters, control panels, and a variety of other products.

"Look at this purchase order, Tony," I said. "Can you believe this; it is for five live goats for a dinner party."

"Yes, they roast the goat in a pit; it is very popular in Arabia, sort of a national dish. The roasted goat is served up on a large platter and everyone at the party helps themselves; it is called a 'goat grab'. I'm sure you'll get invited to one at some point."

"Sounds like an interesting way to dine and a lot of fun," I exclaimed.

"Yes, it is," said Tony. "I've been to several goat grab dinners."

During my tenure at the purchasing department, I reviewed a number of unusual purchase orders. I photocopied one and took it home to show Monica.

"Look at this Monica, this came to me for review today."

It was a purchase order for twenty-five gold Rolex watches with gold bracelets for long service awards. At over eight thousand dollars apiece, the total order was worth over two hundred thousand dollars, and was placed on a local jewellery shop in Al-Khobar.

"Money seems to be no object over here," I exclaimed. "I can't imagine a company in North America spending that amount of money on long service awards."

I tore up the copy of the purchase order and threw it in the trash after Monica had read it.

A few weeks later I received a purchase order for a Boeing 737 aircraft that was an addition to Aramco's fleet. I was getting used to these unusual purchase orders that came by me every once in a while. Very few consumer products are made in Saudi Arabia. Everything has to be purchased from overseas, from very small items to large pieces of equipment and machinery. As a result, thousands of purchase orders are processed every month for all of the many Aramco construction projects. The projects included the building of schools, housing, roads and sea ports, in addition to oil installations.

I had been working in the purchasing department for about four months when I was offered a new part-time position. Gerry Morrow, who was running quality assurance education seminars, asked me if I would like to run the seminars.

"We have to educate the new hires on how to call up the correct inspection and quality assurance procedures when they purchase equipment for their project. Most of them don't have a clue how to do this, and some of the personnel who've been in Arabia for a while can't seem to get it correct either," he explained. "I've been running the seminars for quite a while, and I think I need a change."

"I've never been involved with education seminars," I replied. "Do you think I would be able to do it?"

"Not a problem," Gerry replied. "I'll take you along when I have the next seminar scheduled; you can see exactly what I do and how I teach the program. You can come with me as many times as you need, to get comfortable with it, and then when you're ready you can teach the program and I'll observe."

"Sounds good to me," I replied.

About a week later Gerry contacted me and said that he had a seminar scheduled for Abqaiq, which is about ninety minutes drive from Dhahran.

"We'll leave at 7:00 a.m., as we have to put on the seminar at 9:00 a.m. It takes about thirty minutes to get set up when we get there, so we've lots of time."

I sat at the back of the room observing Gerry and taking notes. The seminar lasted for about forty-five minutes with a question period at the end. It seemed fairly straightforward to me. I felt that I would need to sit in on several seminars before I would be ready to take over from Gerry. I had to become well versed with Aramco's quality assurance procedures so that I wouldn't make any mistakes, and could field the question period with confidence. I had never done any public speaking before, and was a little nervous about standing in front of a room full of people.

I'm dreading the first time, I thought. *I hope I don't make a complete ass of myself in front of a room full of people, or suddenly freeze up, or perhaps worse.*

I accompanied Gerry on three more seminars, and I practised the seminar at home in front of Monica.

"I don't think I'll make any glaring errors now," I said to Monica. "I think I've got it to the point where I'm comfortable with it all."

The following day I told Gerry I would do the next seminar when Gerry had it scheduled.

"I'll go with you and sit at the back of the room and see how you do," Gerry replied.

It was about two weeks later that we set off early one morning for Ras Tanura for my first seminar. It was about an hour-and-a-half drive from Dhahran. I kept going over the seminar in my head to see if I had forgotten anything. I had made some reference notes, which I would keep in front of me, to be sure I wouldn't omit anything.

Gerry was a perfectionist, especially when it came to Aramco procedures; there was no half measure, and it had to be done correctly and to the book.

Gerry and I signed in at the refinery gate, and proceeded to room fifty-one in the administration building where the seminar was scheduled to be held. From our pickup truck, we unloaded ten looseleaf binders containing the sample 175B inspection forms that I would need for the seminar. Also a box containing twenty-five quality assurance manuals, and an overhead projector. The projector and looseleaf binders were set up and made ready for the seminar. The quality assurance manuals were distributed on the trestle tables, one for each attendee to keep. I had my notes placed beside the projector; I didn't want to omit any part of the presentation.

I was very nervous. However, the seminar went well and according to plan. Just after the question period as all the attendees were leaving, an engineer came up to me and said, "I thought you were from the States until you said centrifugal pump instead of centrifical pump, which is how we pronounce it in the United States."

After everyone had cleared the room and we were packing up to leave, Gerry remarked, "I could tell you were a little nervous Mark; I could see your papers shaking from the back of the room. But you did OK; the seminars are yours from now on. You don't need me around; you can handle it just fine."

The purchasing department decided it needed to put on education seminars on Aramco's purchasing procedures, and how to correctly complete a purchase requisition. This was mainly for the new hires who'd just arrived in Arabia. It was also a refresher for the benefit of existing personnel who weren't following procedures correctly. Numerous purchase requisitions were received in the Dhahran Purchasing Department that weren't completed correctly. Beth Somerton in the Dhahran Purchasing Department was assigned the task of developing and presenting the seminars. She contacted me one day and suggested that we put on our seminars together.

"It would be a benefit for both of us if we travelled together and shared a vehicle," she said. "Because women aren't allowed to drive, I would have to have a driver. I would feel much more comfortable travelling with someone I know, rather than with a driver I wouldn't know, and who would be different for every trip. Also, it would provide the engineers and purchasing people attending the seminars a good understanding of how quality assurance and purchasing interact with each other for procurement purposes."

"Sounds like a good idea to me," I said. "It will save us both some organizational time, and provide you with some assistance whilst travelling."

"I appreciate that," she replied."I think we'll work well together as a team."

After a few seminars I lost all nervousness and became comfortable with talking to a group of people. I started to look forward to the next seminar, and to meeting and talking to all the new people. It was a new experience that I grew to enjoy.

This wasn't a full-time job for me or Beth. Over the next few months, Beth and I put on numerous seminars all over Saudi Arabia. We travelled as far as Yanbu by corporate aircraft to the new refinery under construction on the Red Sea. We also travelled to gas plants, gas oil separation plants (GOSPS), refineries and Aramco camps scattered throughout the kingdom. This included Udhailiyah, Safaniyah, Ju'aymah, Abqaiq and Ras Tanura. We always looked forward to going to the Shedgum Gas Plant because the canteen at Shedgum had the best food. They nearly always won the yearly competition for best food. I was very partial to desserts, and would indulge in two or three desserts when we visited Shedgum.

"Not good for my waist," I said to Beth. "But what the hell, we don't eat here every day."

"That's probably a good thing," Beth replied.

CHAPTER 10

The First Holiday

Monica and I were anticipating our one-year anniversary in Saudi Arabia. We were looking forward to our first repatriation, or repat as it was commonly abbreviated. We weren't entitled to a paid holiday until we'd been in the kingdom one complete year. It was a long time to go without a holiday and without leaving the kingdom. After the first year we took two and sometimes three holidays each year.

"Shall we go to Greece?" I asked Monica one day over supper. It was June and it seemed lots of fellow Aramcons were going on short holidays.

"That sounds wonderful." Monica replied, "Perhaps we could take a cruise around the Greek Islands as well; I've always wanted to do that."

"I'll see what is available through the travel agents. I'll also see if anyone is advertising that kind of trip on the Aramco notice board by the commissary," I said.

Two weeks later I had it all booked. Five days in Athens and a cruise around the Greek islands for six days. I had found the trip on the Aramco notice board. It was being organized by someone with a part-time job booking holiday trips. The lady booking the trip told me there would be twenty-three people on the trip, and they were all Aramco families.

I completed the forms for exit and re-entry permits for my family, and submitted them to the Aramco passport office. It takes several weeks for this process, and results in a large blue stamp in your passport marked 'Exit & Re-entry Visa'. Also a stamp that resembles a postage stamp is affixed to the upper centre of the blue stamp. The blue visa stamp indicates that the bearer has to leave the kingdom within a month of the date on the visa, and return within a prescribed date. Blaine had his baby picture in his passport, which was taken when he was about three months old. He was issued a businessman's passport, as were Monica and I. There were insufficient pages in standard passports to contain all the Exit & Re-entry Visas, and stamps of the countries we would eventually visit.

I had never gotten into wine making, but a lot of Aramcons did make their own wine, because alcohol of any description wasn't available in the kingdom. Some of the homemade wines were very good, and others were undrinkable. My diving buddy, Jim McColl, who was from Vancouver, made some very acceptable wine.

"When you're in Greece, pick up a vapour lock, a hydrometer and some yeast," he said to me, "then you'll be able to make your own homemade wine. We make it from Rauch grape juice, which is available at the commissary," he said.

Jim also made his own homemade alcohol with a still he had concocted from a pressure cooker.

"I make the alcohol from sugar," Jim said, "which is also available from the commissary in 25-pound sacks."

I didn't want to get into that, as I thought it far too risky.

The Dhahran hospital provided us with Quinine tablets to give Blaine when we arrived in Athens, as Greece was considered a malaria risk country.

"We'll mash up the pill and put it in some jam," Monica said, "He'll never notice it in the sweet jam."

You can fool a child some of the time, but not all of the time. Monica gave him some jam first which he thought was great. As soon as he received the jam doctored with anti-malaria drug he screwed up his face and spat it out immediately. He wasn't having any of that, thank you very much!

"Now what do we do," said Monica. "If he detects it in jam, he'll detect it in just about anything."

"I think you're right about that," I said. "I guess we don't give it to him." And that's the way it was. Blaine didn't have his anti-malaria pills and we avoided mosquito areas.

The five days in Athens were spent seeing some of the historic sites this ancient city has to offer. We relaxed at tavernas over long lunches, and sampled the local cuisine and Greek wines.

"It's wonderful to live like normal people," Monica remarked as we sat at a sidewalk café, "and not have to worry about showing your bare legs and shoulders. And to have a glass of wine in public!"

I visited a little store that provided the amateur wine maker with all the necessary equipment to make homemade wine. I purchased a vapour lock, hydrometer and three packets of yeast, as my friend Jim had recommended.

After the five days in Athens we boarded a cruise ship at the port of Piraeus for a six-day cruise of the Greek Islands in the Aegean Sea. Piraeus has been the port of Athens since ancient times, and is busy with all the cruise ships, ferries and brisk commercial traffic.

We visited Mykonos, Santorini, Crete, and Rhodes. We were impressed with the beautiful beaches, whitewashed buildings, blue-domed churches, and magnificent antiquities and ruins of ancient civilizations.

I remembered the spectacular physical beauty of Santorini with its winding track up the high steep cliffs. We rode on little donkeys from the old harbour to Fira. The donkeys are extremely adept at negotiating the steep path and steps. They do have a tendency to go very fast and take the bends rather quickly up the 220-metre-long track to Fira. Going up, sharing a saddle with Blaine was no problem for the tough little donkey. Coming back down when we returned to the ship was quite the experience. The donkeys race down the steep path with wild abandon. It was all I could do to hold Blaine in the saddle at what seemed like breakneck speed. Blaine was bouncing up and down along with me, and by the time we reached the harbour, Blaine was fast asleep.

Our cruise ship also made a stop at Istanbul. We visited the Grand Bazaar (covered bazaar), one of the largest and oldest covered markets in the world. A bus trip took us to Ephesus to see the ruins of the old city that's located near the Aegean Sea in modern day Turkey. It was one of the great cities of the Greeks in Asia Minor and home to the Temple of Artemis, one of the Seven Wonders of the ancient World.

Our holiday came and went far too quickly. We soon found ourselves back in Saudi Arabia, going through the customs at Dhahran airport. I put my wine-making supplies in the pocket of a leather coat that I had purchased in Mykonos, and was wearing it through customs.

"They never search your pockets," I told Monica, "so I shouldn't have a problem with the customs finding the supplies."

"You hope," Monica replied.

We cleared customs with the usual search of our cases. All cases were opened, and the contents of one case were dragged out onto the counter. The customs agent went through our belongings meticulously.

"Why you buy this?" the customs official asked me, holding up a souvenir plate that he dragged from a suitcase. It had been carefully packed between clothing to prevent breakage. He dropped it onto the pile of clothes in indignation.

After repacking our belongings that the customs official had so crudely pulled from our cases, we proceeded to the exit door. Our porter was pushing a handcart containing our luggage. I was carrying Blaine who was asleep on my shoulder. Just before the exit, a customs official checked our bags for the chalk mark that indicated we'd been through the baggage check. He then grabbed my coat pocket in which I had the wine-making yeast safely packed.

"What's this?" he asked, as my heart sank. I reacted quickly.

"Food, food," pointing to Blaine's mouth.

"OK" he said. "Go ahead."

We were soon on our way out of the customs area and on our way to a friend's car waiting outside the building.

"I thought you said they never search your pockets!" Monica said to me when we were leaving the airport.

"Well that's what the guys at work told me. I guess they were wrong about that," I conceded.

"You were lucky Mark, you could have landed in jail for a bag of yeast, and then what would we have done!"

I realized the stupidity of taking such a risk, and decided never to do anything like that again.

What an idiot I was, I thought.

CHAPTER 11

Move to Dhahran

It was about two years before I had enough housing points to move to temporary in-camp housing in Dhahran.

"It will seem like moving from the desert to civilisation," Monica remarked when I came home with the news that we were moving. North Camp had been better than the condo at Sea View, as it was much closer to Dhahran. But because there are no trees or vegetation of any kind to provide shade, the heat and blowing sand were unrelenting at times. Our trailer had good air-conditioning, but you could burn your hand on the steel latch of the trailer door during the summer months. Everything outside the trailer got so hot that you had to be very careful what you touched.

"I'll be glad to move out of 'Moon Base Charley'," Monica said. "It can't come soon enough for me. It will be so nice not to have to rely on the buses every day. It will save me a lot of time," she said.

Our new home in Dhahran was a two-bedroom semi-detached bungalow constructed of concrete blocks. I estimated it was about twenty-five years old. The location was good for Blaine, as it was opposite a children's playground. It had a small grassed yard at the front with two large palm trees for shade. The yard was surrounded by a thick bushy perimeter hedge with a small wooden entry gate. It wasn't anything fancy, but was clean and in good condition inside with a reasonably sized living room and dining room and adequate kitchen space. There was a serving hatch between the kitchen and dining room, and the stove was gas. The location was also good for Monica. It was only a few blocks from the hospital, and within walking distance of the commissary and swimming pool. It would make Monica's life much easier as everything was accessible without having to rely on buses.

"We'll have to get some furniture and carpets," Monica said.

"I think we'll rent furniture from Aramco," I replied. "The rental cost is very reasonable, and we'll not have to worry about selling furniture when we leave Arabia. If you've time tomorrow or Wednesday, go down to the furniture warehouse and pick out what we need. Don't forget to get a fridge and washer and dryer, as I noticed we don't have those appliances. You can phone me at work if you've any questions when you're making the selection. I think Dee Wilmingdon works at the warehouse; you remember her, Ron's wife. We met them during our orientation in Houston. They're from Calgary."

"Yes I remember Dee," Monica said. "I saw her in the commissary about a month ago. She said to give her and Ron a call and come and visit sometime."

"Do you realize that it will only take me about five minutes to get to work from our new home? I won't have to get up so early. Now that will be nice!"

Ten days later the keys to our new home were released to me. We moved in on the following weekend. Our move from North Camp didn't take long as we didn't have any furniture to worry about. Just the few possessions that we'd brought from Canada—the same belongings we'd moved from Sea View—and a few souvenirs. Monica had arranged for our rental furniture to be delivered to our new home the day before the move. It was all there and in the appropriate rooms when we moved in, in typical Aramco efficiency. Aramco had also repainted the interior of the house, as was normal procedure when new tenants take over a dwelling.

"It feels more like a proper home," Monica remarked, as we were hanging up our clothes in the closet. "It is so nice to have all this extra room. I was beginning to get claustrophobia in our trailer in North Camp."

"I see that Blaine has already made himself a new friend with the next door neighbour's dog," I exclaimed.

"Yes, his name is Lucius," Monica replied. "He is very friendly, and seems to get along well with Blaine. It's so nice that Blaine can play outside in the garden, and we don't have to worry about him wandering off somewhere."

We soon settled in our new home, and found it a big improvement over North Camp. Dhahran seemed like a little California town.

"It's so nice to have sidewalks, green grass, shrubs and trees," Monica remarked over supper one evening. "It takes me no time at all to go to the pool with Blaine, and the best part is that I don't have to wait for a bus afterwards. By the way, Mark, I was talking to Dee Wilmingdon on the phone today. She phoned to see if all our rental furniture was okay. She invited us over for supper on Friday, so I said we would look forward to that."

Dee's husband Ron is a geophysicist and was seconded to Aramco from Imperial Oil in Calgary. He was nearing retirement, and took the opportunity to spend a few years in Arabia so that he and his wife could do some travelling. As he was a high grade code employee, he had lots of housing points. As a result they moved directly into permanent housing in Dhahran as soon as they arrived in Arabia.

On Friday afternoon, which is the weekend in Arabia, Monica strapped Blaine into his pushchair, and we walked over to Ron and Dee's home. We stopped at the children's playground across the street from our home on the way so that Blaine could get some exercise.

Ron and Dee's home was like any home you would find in North America. It was light brown stucco with a tiled roof, and had an attached single garage. The front garden had a small patio surrounded by a grassed area with flower beds and shrubs. It had two small palm trees about ten feet tall towards the front of the garden. A low stucco wall with a wrought-iron entry gate surrounded the garden. Ron's Cadillac was parked in the driveway.

I rang the bell and Dee came to the door.

"Come in, come in! It's good to see you both and little Blaine. Gosh, he sure has grown since I saw him last. I love your hat, Blaine. Where did you get that?"

"That's Blaine's railway worker's hat that Danielle Fenton, a friend we met in orientation, made for him,"

Monica replied. "It's ideal for keeping the sun off his face."

Ron and Dee's home was really nicely decorated inside with lots of Middle Eastern memorabilia, and several Egyptian rugs on the floor of the lounge. Dee had an organ against one wall with a metronome to one side of its polished top surface, and sheet music in the music stand.

"I didn't know you played the organ," I exclaimed. "Have you been playing long?"

"About 25 years," Dee replied. "I find it very relaxing, and get a lot of enjoyment from it. I'll play something for you later on if you like."

"That would be great," I replied. "We would love to hear you play."

Ron poked his head around the corner of the kitchen and said he would be with us in a few moments.

"He's just preparing some appetizers," Dee said. "He loves to fiddle around in the kitchen; he quite often cooks our supper."

A few minutes later Ron came out of the kitchen. He had a large plate of assorted veggies and dip, pretzels, cheese, pita bread and hummus, which he placed on the coffee table.

"Now what can I get you folks to drink?" he asked. "We've various soft drinks and juices, and I have some Sid if you would like something stronger."

Monica said she would have orange juice, and said Blaine would have the same.

"I've heard about Sid," I said. "What do you normally have with it?"

"We drink it with tonic," Ron replied. "Would you like to try some?"

"Sure I'll give it a try," I replied. "Do you run a still?" I asked Ron.

"Not really," he replied. "A friend has a still and sometimes when he is making a batch I help him out. I don't think I would want to have one myself. It's too risky."

"I agree," I replied. "I think I might try my hand at wine making, but that's about it for me."

"We're really enjoying Dhahran," Dee said. "It is giving us a chance to do some travelling, and that's the main reason for us being here. I like my job at the Aramco furniture warehouse as it gives me something to do, and the extra money for travelling always comes in handy."

"I think I might try and get a part-time job at the hospital as a physiotherapist now that we're in camp," Monica said. "I can walk to work from where we live now, as the hospital is only a few blocks away. I'll have to get a babysitter for Blaine, but that shouldn't be a problem. I've not applied yet. In the next few weeks I think I'll go and see the head of Physiotherapy at the hospital, to see if they have a position available."

Ron brought our drinks on a tray, and handed me my Sid with a can of tonic to go along with it.

"The Sid is strong, Mark, so you may want to put lots of tonic with it. If you don't like it, I'll get you something else."

We sat and chatted for a while and munched on the appetizers. Blaine sat on Monica's knee and munched on a carrot, but after eating half of it, decided that was enough.

"How do you like your drink?" Ron asked me.

"I like it," I replied. "It is strong as you said, and has an unusual taste, a little bit like Tequila I would say.

By the way I like your Cadillac," I exclaimed. "Is it a new one?"

"No," Ron replied, "it is a year old. I bought it from a fellow in the office who was retiring and going home to the States. He sold it to me for a good price, so I couldn't pass it up."

"I don't have a car yet," I said. "I can use the company truck, which I have for work, but Aramco restricts the use of it to company business. I do use it occasionally for personal use. But it is risky, especially if I were to get into a traffic accident. So I don't use it very often, mostly around camp if I need to. If you ever decide to sell the Cadillac let me know as I may be interested in buying it from you."

"Dinner's ready," Dee announced as she brought in a pork roast from the kitchen. "We're having pork with roast potatoes, brussels sprouts and peas, and I've made some Yorkshire puddings. Do you folks like Yorkshire pudding?

"We love it," I replied. "We haven't had Yorkshire pudding for a long time."

After we were seated, Ron opened a bottle of homemade wine and filled everyone's glass.

"This is like being at home," Monica remarked. "I like your wine Ron, it goes great with the roast pork. Do you make a lot of wine?"

"Not a lot," Ron replied, "just enough for Dee and me."

"How do you make it?" I asked.

"It's made from Rauch grape juice which is available from the Aramco commissary. It's quite easy to make, just takes a little time."

After supper Dee entertained everyone by playing some tunes on the organ, and she sat Blaine on her lap so that he could thump the keys and pretend that he was playing. He thought it was wonderful!

During the evening, Ron asked me if I could help him run a TV cable from their upstairs bedroom to the adjoining second bedroom. He wanted to use the second bedroom as a small sitting room and office. Ron said he would climb up in the attic, but needed my help to push the cable through a hole he had drilled in the ceiling. Then pull it back down again through a hole he had drilled in the ceiling of the spare bedroom.

"I want somewhere to watch TV when Dee is playing the organ," Ron said.

"Any time," I replied.

"Thanks Mark, I appreciate your help."

For Monica and me it was like being back home again. Ron and Dee were lucky to go into permanent housing, as they had most of the comforts of a North American home. When Monica and I returned to the starkness of our temporary home that evening, it was like stepping back to the reality of a lower standard of living. We didn't have the creature comforts of a traditional western home like Ron and Dee. We would in time; we just had to wait a while.

A few weeks went by and Monica and I became accustomed to living on camp. Monica was getting a little bored as she seemed to have a lot of free time on her hands without the travelling from North Camp. One day over supper she said she was thinking of looking into getting a job in the physiotherapy department of the hospital.

"It would just be part-time if they have an opening, just the mornings or afternoons, depending what's available. I would have to get a babysitter for Blaine, but that wouldn't be a problem I'm sure."

"Have you checked into it at all?" "I asked.

"No I've not, but I'll go into the physiotherapy department next week and see what's available."

The phone rang and Monica picked it up as she was already on her feet putting the supper dishes in the serving hatchway to the kitchen.

"It's for you," she said. "I think it may be Ron." Monica handed me the phone.

"Hi Ron, how are you folks doing?"

"Hi Mark," Ron replied. "I'm wondering if you would be interested in buying my Cadillac? You'd expressed an interest when you were over for supper a few weeks ago."

"I don't think I can afford it just yet," I replied. "I thought perhaps you would be keeping it for a couple of years before selling it. Why are you selling it now?"

"We've had a family emergency at home," Ron replied. "So we're leaving to go home."

"You won't be coming back?" I asked.

"No we won't be."

"Well, we're really sorry to hear that. We're going to miss you and Dee."

"It's one of those things," Ron replied. "Can't be helped."

"When are you leaving?" I asked.

"Thursday evening," Ron replied. "We catch the 11:30 p.m. flight from Dhahran to Frankfurt."

"That's only three days away!" I exclaimed. "I hope we'll see you and Dee before you go. Do you have anyone taking you to the airport on Thursday?"

"No we don't," Ron replied.

"I'll take you to the airport. Why don't you come over to our place for supper on Thursday evening, and after supper I'll take you to the airport."

"Sounds good," Ron replied. "I appreciate you doing that for us."

"That's the least I can do Ron. If you like, you can have a shower at our place just before I take you to the airport."

"Thanks Mark," Ron replied. "I'll be talking to you before Thursday, bye for now." And he hung up the phone.

I told Monica what had transpired, and said I found it strange that they were leaving so quickly.

"It is hard to believe that they won't be coming back," Monica said. "I'll miss them both."

On Thursday, Ron and Dee came around for supper at 4:00 p.m. as planned. They had one small carry-on bag each. The rest of their belongings and all their furniture had already been packed and shipped. They seemed very nervous, and didn't offer any further information about the family emergency that was the reason for their sudden departure from Saudi Arabia. Monica and I didn't ask them about their family emergency. We thought that if they wanted to discuss it they would have said something. Nothing further was said by either of them.

"We're so sorry to see you both go," Monica told them over supper. "We're going to miss seeing you both. Do you think you'll come back again someday?"

"No, we won't be coming back again," Dee said, with tears in her eyes. "We'd hoped to do a lot more travelling. It was the main reason for us coming to Arabia, but that's the way things go. You'll have to come and see us in Calgary when you come back on repat."

"We'll definitely do that," I replied.

There was no further discussion about their leaving, as both Monica and I got the impression that they didn't want to discuss it further.

After supper, Ron and Dee took a shower to freshen up before their long journey home. I drove them to the Dhahran airport in my company truck at 8:00 p.m. I had received permission from my supervisor to use the truck, as I wasn't supposed to use it for private use. There were hugs for Monica as they left the house, and Dee was very upset and almost in tears again.

It was a quiet twenty-five minute drive to the airport. Hardly a word was spoken. I could detect that Ron and Dee were very nervous and upset for some reason, but I didn't know why. Perhaps it was just because of their premature exit from the country, or perhaps they were just worried about the family problems. In my mind I tried to put myself in their position to try and understand how they felt, but something still didn't add up to me.

When they arrived at the airport, Ron and Dee quickly stepped out of my truck and said a hurried goodbye. They promised to write when they returned home. They turned and made their way into the airport and were gone.

About a month later Monica and I received a letter from Ron and Dee.

Dear Mark and Monica,
We arrived safely to our home in Calgary, and felt that we owed you an explanation for our hurried departure from Dhahran.
As you know I didn't run a still whilst I was in Arabia. However, I did help a friend run his still to make Sid. Neither I nor my friend sold Sid as we only made it for

our own consumption. One day I took a bottle of Sid into work to give to a friend in another office.

I gave the bottle that I had in a paper bag to my office assistant, and asked him to take it to the floor above and give it to Colin. The office assistant, who was a young Saudi, gave it to Khalid (a Saudi national) by mistake, and Khalid reported it to Aramco Internal Affairs.

Within hours I was told that I was fired, and Aramco would be packing my belongings and shipping me back to Canada immediately. We were very upset and nervous for the three days that it took Aramco to pack all our furniture and belongings, and to exit the country. We were in constant fear of being arrested and thrown in jail.

We didn't relax until we were on the plane and it had finally lifted off the ground. Then we knew we were safe from the Saudi police. We were really sorry to be leaving Saudi Arabia under these conditions. We will miss you and all the friends we made during our short tenure in the kingdom.

Please come and see us when you're back to Calgary on repatriation.

Love and best wishes,

Your friends, Ron and Dee

CHAPTER 12

Sid Diqui

In the early years of Aramco, things were much different than those of today, according to some of the old timers in Dhahran. Some people have spent their entire working lives in the kingdom, and it is not uncommon to meet third generation Aramcons.

When Dhahran Camp was for expatriate employees only, Dhahran was less restrictive in many ways. If an employee wanted to run a still to make alcohol, a stainless steel still could be purchased from special order sales. It came with a book, called the Blue Flame, on how to operate the still. Aramco stopped selling stills many years ago. However, there are a number of stainless steel stills that remain in operation today, having been sold and handed down as expatriates returned home.

Some expatriates manufacture their own stills, as they aren't difficult to fabricate. Jim McColl, my diving buddy, fashioned his still out of a pressure cooker. Jim made alcohol for his own consumption only. The pressure cooker, although slow and of a low production rate, was adequate for his needs.

There were a number of people in Dhahran running a still, and selling the illegal alcohol called Siddiqui or Sid for short.

The Saudi men often use the word Siddiq, when they talk to you and don't know your name. They call you Siddiq, which means my friend. The word seems to have originated from Africa where it means "Friend Righteous." Some of the Saudi Arabians originated from Africa. So the name for the illicit alcohol is essentially "my friend." In Arabic it also means "truthful," and is an Islamic term that is given as an honorific title to certain individuals.

An enterprising Aramcon decided to make and sell T-shirts with 'Sid Diqui is My Friend' printed on them.

Some expatriates found making illegal alcohol a lucrative business. They could make lots of extra money in addition to their Aramco salary. This is highly illegal and the penalty if caught by the Saudi police is a long jail term. Nevertheless, there were a few expatriates who thought it was worth the risk when Sid sold for about $350 to $400 per gallon uncut. Most drinkers would cut it 50% with water, or add lots of mix because it is about 90% alcohol.

It wasn't uncommon to see someone buying 22-pound bags of sugar from the Aramco commissary on their way home from work. In that quantity it wasn't for making cookies or cakes! In all the new homes that Aramco built in Dhahran Hills, a stillroom is built onto one side of the garage. It is called a utility room. However, it is equipped with a floor drain, a shelf for the still, 220-volt power outlet and an exhaust fan. Aramco is very safety conscious and wouldn't want someone running a still in the kitchen, hence the reason for the stillroom.

On a few occasions when Monica and I were out for an evening walk with Blaine, we would smell the sweet odor of mash from a still wafting over the back yard wall of a home into the back alley. It was an unmistakable odor.

* * * * *

When I went into work one morning, my supervisor informed me that one of the Aramco off-shore barges had a problem with some of its instrumentation. They wanted me to visit the ARB-1 barge to see what the problem was, and make a report on my findings.

"I've made arrangements for you to fly out to the ARB-1 barge next Tuesday," my supervisor Dave Hansen informed me. "A helicopter will pick you up at the helipad by the golf course at 7:00 a.m., so don't be late. Take the office camera. You can take some photographs to add to your report."

I had never been up in a helicopter before so I was looking forward to the trip.

It would be a day out doing something different, I thought.

A few minutes later Dave came back into my office and said he had a new job for me starting in two weeks' time.

"We're getting rid of some of our servorgs," Dave said. "We're cancelling Dennis McBride's contract at the end of the month so we need a replacement for him. At the present time, Dennis is looking after welding and coating work at the Al-Qahtani Company in Dammam. They double joint forty-foot lengths of pipe for cross-country pipelines. They also have a Fusion Bonded Epoxy (FBE) coating plant where they coat the pipe before it is shipped to the job site. Starting on Sunday, I want you to tag along with Dennis when he goes to Al-Qahtani, and get familiar with what he does out there. Get him to introduce you to all the people that he works with at that plant so that you can take over when he leaves at month's end."

This came as quite a shock to me as I knew nothing about coating pipe, but I had done welding inspection in Canada. That part I could handle.

I told Jim DeAngelo about my conversation with Dave and my new assignment, and the fact that I didn't know anything about pipe coating.

"Don't worry about it, Mark. Just go along with it and learn all you can; they'll send you to school and make you an expert which will be another feather in your cap."

I wasn't convinced, but realized that I didn't have a lot of choice. It wasn't forever, so what the heck. I would probably find it interesting as long as it didn't get repetitious.

Austin Barton poked his head into my office to ask how things were going.

"Jim and I are doing fine, Austin. How are you doing with your video club?" I asked.

"It's going great. I've over seven hundred video movies now, and it is growing by nine movies per week. I'll bring you in a title list if you're interested in renting movies from time to time."

"Thanks Austin," I replied. "I've just bought a video player so would definitely rent a few movies from you."

I had another quick cup of coffee before going over to the Purchasing department to settle in for the day reviewing purchase orders. I had been working in the purchasing department for about eight months, and I was finding it a little repetitious. However, the purchasing office was air conditioned so it was a comfortable place to work. I had a lot of interaction by phone with engineers and purchasing people from other Aramco camps and facilities scattered around the kingdom.

I was still running the quality assurance seminar which took me out of the office from time to time. It provided a nice break from office work. It was now July, and not uncommon for the temperature to be well over one hundred degrees Fahrenheit all the time, sometimes reaching one hundred and fifteen at midday. I carried a two-gallon thermos-type water container in the car. It was packed with ice and water before I left Dhahran on a trip, just in case I had car troubles. My biggest worry was getting into a car accident and being thrown in jail.

Tuesday rolled around and I was up early to make sure I wasn't late at the helipad.

It was going to be another hot day, I thought, as I stood waiting beside my truck in the small car park beside the helipad. The sun was a red ball of fire as it crept up from the horizon in a haze of dust. I noticed that whenever I flew over the kingdom I could never see a clear horizon. The blue sky seemed to sink into a line of dust before reaching the ground, which made me wonder how clean the air was that I was breathing. I glanced at my watch—7:10 a.m. and no sign of the chopper. Perhaps the pilot had been misinformed about the day. A few more minutes went by in silence, and then I heard the familiar thrashing of the rotor blades way off in the distance. I couldn't see the aircraft, and wondered if it was a chopper headed somewhere else. The thrashing of the rotor blades grew louder, and a tiny speck became visible from out of the sun as the little helicopter slowly approached the helipad. I locked my truck and made my way up the tarmac path to the helipad. As the chopper approached the pad the rotor blades kicked up a dust storm of sand from the desert floor surrounding the pad. The pilot dropped down onto the pad and throttled off the engine, and waved for me to approach the chopper. I grabbed the door handle and quickly climbed on board, and strapped myself in with the seatbelts.

"Where are you headed?" the pilot yelled over the clatter of the rotor blades.

"ARB-1," I replied.

"Where's that?" the pilot asked.

"Don't you know?" I asked.

"I've no idea," the pilot replied.

Well this is a good start, I thought. *Now what do we do.*

"Don't worry about it," the pilot replied. "We'll find it. I've got a map," and he pulled out a large map and laid it open.

He pointed to a spot on the map that was north and east of Dhahran, and a little way off shore.

"I think the ARB-1 is about there," he indicated with his finger. "We'll go take a look."

He folded the map and placed it between his legs, increased the engine speed and lifted off from the helipad. I had a bird's eye view of Dhahran for the first time as we rapidly gained altitude over the golf course and the older part of the camp. We headed northward towards the town of Dammam, and the coastline came in sight.

"My name's Jesse," the pilot yelled over the noise of the engine, as he extended his hand to me.

"I'm Mark," I replied as I shook Jessie's hand.

"Have you been in the kingdom long?" Jessie asked.

"About two years," I replied. "How about you?"

"Two and a half years."

"Where were you before that?" I asked.

"I worked for Uncle Sam for ten years, which is where I learned to fly choppers. I did several tours in Nam flying helicopter gunships."

I realized I was in good hands with a very experienced pilot who probably had a lot of hours logged in very dangerous conditions.

This trip was probably like a Sunday school picnic for him, I thought.

We followed the highway to Dammam and then north across the town and picked up the highway to Ras Tanura. We followed the highway for a while and then headed northeast towards the coast.

"Looks like we've a calm sea today," Jesse said. "That will make it easy to drop on the helipad of the ARB-1. It can be a little tricky if there is a rough sea or a swell, or lots of wind."

We followed the coastline for a while and I noticed a few dhows that I assumed were local fishermen, but saw no other vessels. Then Jesse headed further out to sea where he thought the ARB-1 should be located.

"Looks like a vessel a little further out to the east," Jesse said. "I think that may be her."

As we came closer to the vessel we could see it was a working barge with a helipad. Jesse radioed to the ARB-1 for permission to land, and dropped altitude and circled the barge. He put the little helicopter down on the deck with the precision of a surgeon, and throttled back the engine and shut it down. After we climbed down from the helipad, Jesse said he would be in the canteen when I was ready to return to Dhahran.

It took me about four hours to complete my inspection of the instrumentation they were concerned about. Most of the problems resulted from lack of service or damage, which I documented and photographed where I was able.

I found Jesse in the canteen drinking a cup of coffee and reading a magazine.

"I'm going to grab some lunch and then we can head back to Dhahran. Have you eaten?" I asked.

"Yep, had a steak sandwich about an hour ago. Try the berry pie, Mark; it is really good."

About an hour later we made our way up to the helipad and climbed on board the chopper, and were quickly airborne. I snapped a few pictures of the ARB-1 before we headed back to Dhahran. Not long after we were overland, Jesse asked me if I would like to see one of the King's palaces.

"Yes I would," I replied. "Do we go near it on our return?" I asked.

"It is due west of here so we can fly over it without really going out of our way. We'll then head south back to Dhahran."

The palace was out in the desert and from what I could see there didn't seem to be any activity in the compound. It looked impressive, and I wondered how often the King visited this palace.

Probably not often, I thought.

Jesse banked the chopper and flew partway around the palace so I could get some pictures before he headed south.

"We have to be careful," Jesse said. "We can't make it too obvious that we're circling the palace as we might get reported if there is anyone around."

It was nearly 3:30 p.m. when we touched down onto the helipad in Dhahran. I thanked Jesse for the ride and stepped out of the chopper and headed for my truck.

That was an interesting day, I thought, as I drove down the Golf Course Road into Dhahran. I stopped off at the mail centre to pick up my mail before returning home. There was little point in going to the office for half an hour.

On Wednesday morning when I got to my office, a rumour was spreading around the offices about a still that had apparently exploded in a home in Dhahran Hills. Jim DeAngelo was on the phone when I entered the office that we shared, and was obviously being told the details of the explosion. I could hear bits of the conversation of what had happened.

When Jim hung up the phone he said, "Hey Mark, that was a bad one in the Hills yesterday, did you hear about it?"

"I heard the secretary and Dennis saying something about it when I went to get a cup of coffee," I replied. "But don't know the details of it."

"From what I've been told, one of the engineers who has a home in the Hills was running a still in the still room in his garage. He started running it at lunchtime when he went home for a quick bite to eat. At about three o'clock, he phoned his wife and asked her to go into the stillroom and turn off the still. Apparently when she flipped the power off to the still, there was one hell of an explosion. It blew the garage door off and sent it clean across the street onto the neighbour's lawn. His wife was seriously injured, and suffered burns to seventy percent of her body. She's now in the Dhahran hospital."

"Good god!" I exclaimed.

"When the fire department (which is a volunteer group) arrived, the fire chief, who's British, decided to call it a water heater explosion," Jim said. "It was fortunate that it didn't happen fifteen minutes sooner because the kids walk up that street when school comes out. For sure, some of them would have been injured by the garage door when it blew across the street."

When the wife was stabilized and able to travel, she was flown back to a hospital in the United States. Because the fire chief reported a faulty water heater to be the cause of the explosion, the engineer didn't lose his job, and he continued to work for Aramco.

CHAPTER 13

A New Job

On the following Sunday I was in the office early, as I was going to the Al-Qahtani Company in Dammam with Dennis McBride. I was scheduled to take over monitoring of activities at this plant before Dennis left at the end of the month. Dennis was a young Scotsman about twenty-eight years old, heavily tanned with black curly hair and he had a broad Scot's accent. He knew that I was going to be taking over his job, and wasn't happy about the fact that he was returning to the United Kingdom. Dennis didn't say much to me as we were driving to Dammam in his truck that morning. I got the impression that he resented me taking over his job at Al-Qahtani.

When we arrived at the yard, Dennis stopped at the entrance gate and was immediately recognized by the security guard who waved him through.

"I'll show you around the yard first," Dennis said. "It is a large yard, and I monitor all work activities that take place within this company. My job is to ensure that work complies with the Aramco standards and procedures, which are included in the purchase orders that are placed with this company."

The yard covered an area of about forty acres. It consisted of several large buildings, and outside storage for numerous sizes of pipe for cross-country and undersea pipelines.

"There are four main processes completed here," Dennis said. "Fusion Bonded Epoxy coating of pipe up to fifty-six inches in diameter, abbreviated as FBE. Coat and wrap of cross-country pipelines. Weight coating of pipe for undersea pipelines, and double-joint welding of pipe. As you know, pipe comes in forty-foot lengths. To save some of the on-site welding, Aramco has two forty-foot lengths of pipe welded together at this company. To ship the pipe to the site lay-down area in eighty-foot lengths, they use a tractor with a cradle to support the pipe at the front end. A set of wheels with a cradle supports the pipe at the other end. The pipe becomes the trailer in effect. It seems to work well, but obviously you can't make any tight turns when hauling eighty-foot lengths of pipe."

"The FBE coating facility starts running at 7:00 a.m.," Dennis said, "and most of the workers in this plant are from the Yemen or Pakistan. The supervisors and quality assurance personnel are all from the United Kingdom. You have to be very safety conscious in this plant because they're rolling heavy pipe along pipe racks and onto the conveyor line for coating. If you don't keep an eye on the movement of pipe as you walk along the walkways, you could easily get squashed between two pipes."

We got out of Dennis's truck and walked to the entrance of the FBE coating shop.

"Be very careful in here," Dennis warned. "It can be a dangerous place if you don't keep your guard up at all times."

I could immediately see the implications of his warning. Heavy, eighty-foot lengths of rusty pipe were rolling down a pipe rack towards a wheel abrader in preparation for the blast cleaning process. We walked along a walkway across the pipe rack between the pipes.

"If a pipe rolls towards you while you're on this walkway, get off quick. Keep your eyes and ears open at all times. You don't want to be squashed by a pipe. That wouldn't be good for your health! If you don't have time to get across the walkway, jump off the walkway and duck below it."

Dennis walked towards the first wheel abrader, which cleaned most of the rust and mill scale from the pipe using steel shot. The pipe slowly rotates, travelling along the hydraulic roller conveyor line towards the wheel abrader. The pipe entered the wheel abrader and came out the other end relatively clean.

"The shot will clean the pipe, but it doesn't put an anchor profile on the surface for the coating to adhere to. The pipe travels through a second wheel abrader where it is blasted with a sharp grit. This puts a 1.5 to 3 mils profile (.0015 to.003 inches profile) on the pipe surface to a near-white finish for coating adhesion," Dennis said. "Mil is derived from the Latin word mille and it means one thousand, its measurement is one thousandth of an inch," he added. "They can clean over half-a-million square feet of pipe surface a day," he added. "The pipe is then checked for any surface defects that may affect the coating, and any burrs and slivers are removed by locally grinding. Any pipe that's found not suitable for coating is rejected at this stage."

I followed Dennis along another walkway where he stopped to inspect the pipe surface.

"The pipes are coupled together with couplings so that they form a continuous line on this helix conveyor," Dennis said. "After that, the pipe travels through a series of five induction heaters. It is heated to between four hundred and four hundred and seventy degrees Fahrenheit, before going through the coating booth for coating. The weld area cut back at the ends of each pipe is protected by tape so that it doesn't get coated. The pipe is grounded so that it is negatively charged. The coating, which is in a powder form, is positively charged by an electrode at the spray nozzles. As the powder is sprayed onto the pipe, it attracts to the pipe and melts and forms a coating. The weld cut back tape is then removed. The pipe travels through a water spray to cool it, and in so doing the coating sets hard. After the water spray, the pipe couplings are released. Each individual length of pipe rolls down this rack where it is inspected for thickness and holidays."

"What exactly are holidays?" I asked.

"That's the term they use for a hole in the coating," Dennis replied. "If they find a holiday they clean the area with a file and repair it with a torch and melt stick. The pipe is then stencilled, after which it is taken from the end of the inspection rack and stored in the yard until required by the customer. So that's the FBE coating process," Dennis said.

"I'll take you over to the weight coating machine and show you that process. We can walk over there as it is only about a hundred yards from here."

Although it was only 9:15 a.m., it was starting to get hot. The building we'd just come from, which is not air-conditioned, was extremely warm inside due to the heat generated by the machinery. I was starting to sweat, and felt tired from the heat.

The weight coating machine was a strange looking device, I thought.

Adjacent to it was an eighty thousand ton stockpile of finely crushed iron ore that provides the bulk for the weight coat. Forty-foot lengths of pipe that had already been coated with the coat and wrap process were lifted over by crane from the coat and wrap plant. It was then fed into the weight coating machine. As the pipe revolved past a conveyor belt, concrete was impinged onto the pipe surface along with a band of what looked like wire netting for reinforcement.

"The concrete is very dry as you can see," Dennis added. "It is made from a mixture of cement and iron ore particles. They build it up to a thickness from about two to six inches, depending on the client's requirement, to give the correct negative buoyancy. It adds tremendous weight to the pipe, which allows the pipe to sink to the bottom of the ocean when it is laid from the lay barge. The only purpose of the weight coating is to make the pipe sink to the bottom of the ocean."

I noticed that it only took about four minutes to coat one pipe length.

"As a check on quality, each joint (length of pipe) is weighed to ensure it is within the specified limits. It is then moved to the storage area where it is inspected, and any repairs made, prior to curing and stacking," he explained.

An expatriate worker from the United Kingdom was supervising the weight coating process, and all of the operational personnel were from Yemen or Pakistan. It appeared to be a hot dirty job, with no shade over the process except for a small sunshade over the machine operator's seat. I wondered how they could stay out in the heat all day long. I noticed that they all had a supply of water nearby.

It must be hell when the wind is blowing, I thought.

Dennis and I made our way over to his truck which was like an oven inside. Dennis started the engine and put the AC on full blast. It was good to feel the cold air and have a drink of water from Dennis's water cooler.

"You have to get out of the heat periodically," Dennis said, "when you start working here. You're going to find it very hot and exhausting being out in the heat all day, especially if you're used to being in a building with air-conditioning most of the time."

"I'm sure it will be difficult at first, but I'll become accustomed to it in time," I replied.

Dennis took me on a tour of the coat and wrap pipe coating facility, which was primarily outside but a sunshade roof covered part of the process.

"This was the first coating process to be put into operation. It was installed some twenty years ago along with the weight coating. It is about ten percent of the output for this yard. The surface of the pipe is first blast cleaned by the wheel abrader to your left, to remove the rust and scale. It is then primed to ensure full adhesion of the final coating."

We walked over to the priming station where a black liquid was being sprayed on the pipe surface.

"At this coating station the hot coal tar enamel is applied to the pipe, and at the same time that yellow glass fiber reinforcing is wound onto the pipe, and a coal tar paper outer wrap is also wound on. To ensure consistent quality, the entire surface of the coated pipe is checked for holidays, and samples of the finished coating are checked for thickness."

"It looks like a dirty job," I commented.

"Yes it can be," Dennis replied. "You don't want to get any of that hot coal tar on your clothing as you'll never get it out. Also, as it is applied hot, you have to be careful you don't get any of that black crap on your skin. It will give you a nasty burn."

We stood watching the process for a while, and Dennis did some thickness checks of his own as I stood by watching.

"Looks good," Dennis noted. "You have to check the thickness once in a while to ensure it meets the coating specification requirements. They're a fairly good company so you'll not find too many problems."

We walked back over to Dennis's vehicle which he had left running, so it was nice and cool inside.

"We'll go over to the double joint shop and I'll show you that process," Dennis said, as he shifted the truck into gear.

The double jointing shop looked like quite a new building and was open at both ends, and appeared to be about eighty yards long. A pipe rack ran the full length of the building, and a front-end loader was placing forty-foot lengths of thirty-inch diameter pipe onto the racks.

"There are five welding stations in this building," Dennis said, "and they can double joint two forty-foot pipes from eight inches in diameter up to sixty-four inches in diameter. For the smaller pipe sizes up to twenty-two inches in diameter, the weld bevel is cleaned using a combined grit-blasting machine and rotary wire brush. They also have hydraulic end-facing machines to cut the weld bevels in preparation for welding for the larger pipe sizes. After the weld prep is done, the pipe is mechanically moved to the first welding station, where, after it is lined up with pneumatic clamps, the root pass is welded. The pipe is then rolled to the second and third welding stations where the fill and cap welds are added."

"All the welders are from Texas, and they work on a thirty-day rotation. They use Flux Cored Arc Welding (FCAW), Metal Inert Gas (MIG) or Submerged-arc Welding (SAW) welding process. At present they're using Submerged-arc."

We moved along to the next two welding stations where the internal weld was being completed.

"For pipe over twenty-four inches in diameter, welding is completed by a welder inserted into the pipe on a boom. On sixteen-inch to twenty-inch pipe the internal weld is completed by the use of a TV-monitored remote head."

We moved further along to the inspection station where all welds are subjected to one hundred percent X-ray.

"After the film has been exposed, it is processed automatically on site in the radiographic room on your right. The results are available within minutes, before the pipe joint leaves the building. A British company supplies the radiographic crew, and their radiographic assistants are from the Philippines. This process not only reduces the number of field welds by half, it also reduces the field weld coating cost by half. In addition, it contributes to a substantial savings in the cost of transportation," Dennis added. "You've now seen all the processes that are completed at this plant."

"How long have you been working here?" I asked."

"About fourteen months," Dennis replied, "but it seems a lot longer than that for some reason."

Dennis took me into the radiographic room where the film was processed and read. He introduced me to the two technicians who were working in this small, nice and cool air-conditioned building. Dennis sat down and reviewed some of the film that had been processed.

"I generally do a sample check on the weld quality two or three times per shift," Dennis said. "I rarely find any problems as these guys do a good job and are very conscientious."

He reviewed the reader log for the shift, and noticed there had been three anomalies so far that morning that had been identified for repair.

"See you later," Dennis said, as we exited the radiographic room.

I was experienced with welding inspection so I didn't have any concerns in that regard. However, I knew very little about coatings and their inspection, and what Dennis had just shown me was all new to me.

"I would like you to give me a list of all the Aramco specifications and standards that apply to the work that's being completed by this company," I advised Dennis.

"No problem," Dennis replied. "When we get back to the office I'll make a list for you. Why do you need that?" he asked.

"If I'm going to inspect the work at this company, I will need to be conversant with the Aramco standards and specifications that form part of the procurement documents for the coating and welding work at this facility," I added.

"You won't find any problems here," Dennis replied. "I keep a pretty close eye on what goes on, and I very rarely find any problems with this company's work."

"That's good to hear," I replied. "We should probably head back to Dhahran, as I see it is 11:30 a.m. and I have a meeting at the office at one."

We walked back through the welding shop to Dennis's truck, which was parked in the shade but was like an oven inside when we got in. The drive back to Dhahran was uneventful, except for one incident. The driver of a Cadillac cut in in front of him. Dennis had to drive into the desert on the side of the road to avoid a head-on collision with oncoming traffic on the narrow two-lane highway.

"I've never had an accident out here," Dennis said, "but I've come close to it a few times. I sure won't miss these driving conditions when I get back home to the United Kingdom."

When we arrived at the office it was lunchtime. Most of the office personnel were either relaxing with a sandwich and coffee or had gone to the dining hall for lunch.

Jim DeAngelo was sitting in his swivel chair with his feet resting on the corner of the desk reading a newspaper.

"How goes it Mark?" he asked as I entered the office.

"Good," I replied. "I've just been on a tour of the Al-Qahtani plant with Dennis. That's quite an operation. Have you been to that plant, Jim?"

"Yes I have," Jim replied. "I hear he is opening up another plant for internal coating on the other side of Dammam. Did Dennis mention that to you?"

"No he didn't," I replied. "Perhaps he didn't know about it."

"Maybe," replied Jim.

I took out my lunch from my desk drawer, and took my cup to the office next door to get a coffee. When I returned, Austin Barton was talking to Jim about his videotape club.

"Aramco seems to have a problem with my tape club," he was saying. "They said there is a parking problem in the road where I live. It seems that some of my neighbors have complained. They have nowhere to park when they come home from work because so many people are parked in the road outside my house collecting tapes from my club. They said I have to do something about it, as it can't continue. I'm not sure what to do at the present time as I don't want to close it down."

"I hope you don't have to close it," Jim replied. "I rent a lot of movies from you because the movies on TV are cut so bad that they aren't worth watching. Annette and I were watching Dallas the other night, and it was cut from a one-hour show to thirty-five minutes. Every time there was a kiss or a swimming pool scene with someone in a swimsuit, they cut it. It was cut so bad that you couldn't follow the story. I don't have any suggestions for you, Austin, but I hope you find a solution."

"I will," Austin replied. "But I have to find a way out of this quickly as Aramco only gave me ten days to sort it out."

I was listening to all this, and when Austin left our office, I discussed Austin's problem with Jim.

"Austin's tape club must have gotten much bigger than he had anticipated."

"I think it has," Jim replied. "He is making lots of money from that club, so he is not going to shut it down. He'll find a way to resolve the problem I'm sure."

After lunch I had a meeting with my supervisor Dave Hansen.

"How did it go at Al-Qahtani?" Dave asked. "Did Dennis show you around and introduce you to the people you'll be working with?"

"Yes he did," I replied. "I don't have a problem with the welding side of things, that's fairly straightforward. However, I don't know a lot about the coating processes at that plant so it is going to be a learning curve for me in that regard."

"Don't worry about it Mark, we'll get you into some training courses. I would recommend that you join the local chapter of the National Association of Corrosion Engineers, NACE, so that you can attend their monthly meetings. NACE puts on training courses in Dhahran from time to time, and I hear they're very good."

"I'll do that," I replied.

"Dennis hasn't been doing that great a job at Al-Qahtani. That's one of the reasons we're putting an Aramco inspector in that plant rather than a servorg. We need someone who'll keep a close eye on that plant. It does millions of dollars' worth of work for the pipeline divisions, and we can't afford to have things go wrong."

"Mark, I've got you a new truck as you're going to need your own vehicle. You'll need it all day every day to go to Al-Qahtani. You can pick it up at this office in the morning. Also, you don't have to come into the office every day unless you've other business to attend to. You can go directly from home in the mornings, and return home directly from Al-Qahtani which will save you some time. If we need you for some reason, we'll phone you at home, or phone you at Al-Qahtani. Do you have any questions?" Dave asked.

"Not at the moment," I replied. "But if I think of anything, I'll come and see you."

I returned to my office and found the list of Aramco specifications and standards from Dennis sitting on my office chair.

For the remainder of the afternoon, I made copies of all the specifications and standards on Dennis's list. I sat reading them and making notes of points I wanted to review when I was next at the Al-Qahtani plant.

The following morning I picked up my new truck from the office and headed out to Dammam and the Al-Qahtani coating yard. I signed in at the gate as the security guard didn't recognize me, and drove over to the FBE coating shop. I noticed that Dennis had parked his truck at the entrance to the welding shop, and he was leaning against the front of the truck talking to the weld shop supervisor.

I attached the FBE coating specification to my clipboard, and walked through the shop checking off the specification as I verified points in the process. At the quality assurance (QA) office I met with the QA supervisor James Henderson, who was checking coating adhesion and conducting bend tests on two test straps. James was a tall, overweight Englishman with a strong North Country accent. He had a belly that hung over the leather belt that held up his blue jeans, and wore a T-shirt with Sunderland Football Club written across the chest.

"Morning," he greeted me. "You must be the new Aramco inspector that Dennis was telling me about. Sorry to hear that Dennis is leaving. He's a good man."

"Yes I'm taking over from Dennis. My name is Mark Carlile," I said extending my hand to James, who acknowledged it grasping my hand in his chubby hand and shaking it vigorously.

"We do the QA tests in this office, Mark, so feel free to witness the tests or review the test results any time you wish."

"Thanks," I replied. "I appreciate that."

I completed my review of the FBE coating process, and then completed the same type of review with the coat and wrap and weight coating processes. It was another hot day and I made frequent trips back to my truck for water, which was starting to get tepid in the hot vehicle.

Oh well at least it will keep me hydrated, I thought.

* * * * *

Several weeks passed by, and for me it was a learning curve in an aspect of engineering that I knew little about. I joined the local chapter of NACE and started attending their monthly dinner meetings at the local Ramada Hotel. It was a good opportunity to meet with many of the Aramco coating specialists and pipeline engineers, who were involved with the laying of the pipe that was coated at Al-Qahtani. The meetings generally concluded with a technical presentation by a guest speaker on some aspect of coating, which I found enlightening. I found them a friendly group of people, who always had time to answer the questions I frequently had. I made many acquaintances who I could turn to if needed, and I was invited to join the weekly meetings of the pipeline groups, who were responsible for laying pipe all over Arabia.

I remember the first meeting I attended with the Northern Area Pipeline Group. As I was entering the conference room, a young fellow introduced himself and asked me my name and department. I chatted to him for a few minutes, and learned that his name was Derek. He was from North Carolina, and his family members were tobacco farmers. He said he was the assistant to the project manager. When the meeting was about to start, Derek stood up and introduced the twenty-five people seated around the conference table by name and department, and he did it from memory. I was impressed. The fellow seated next to me turned to me and said, "He does that at all our meetings, it is kinda his party piece. I wish I had a memory like that."

"Me too," I replied.

I had been working at the pipe-coating terminal in Dammam for several months, and was beginning to feel confident with the new knowledge and experience I was gaining. I was starting to meet a lot of people who were involved in the coating industry.

I usually left home at 7:00 a.m., and arrived at the Al-Qahtani plant at 7:30 a.m. It was a Tuesday, and I had just arrived at the plant to begin my daily monitoring of activities. When I walked into the FBE coating shop, I noticed that the coating conveyor line was shut down, and there was no activity to be seen. As I walked up to the glass fronted QA office, I saw James Henderson sitting at his desk with a glum look on his face. I walked into the office and said, "Hi James, how come you're shut down?"

He looked at me with a blank stare, and said nothing for a few seconds, then he said, "We won't be running today, Mark, so you may as well go back to Dhahran."

"Why is that?" I asked.

"We had a bad accident here early this morning. The little Yemeni worker, who takes off the cut-back tape from the pipe after it comes out of the spray booth, got caught between the pipe and the conveyor rollers and was crushed to death."

"Oh my god," I exclaimed. "I'm so sorry to hear that. I'm shocked."

"We're all deeply saddened," James said. "He was a nice fellow who was just trying to make money to send back to his family in Yemen." James had tears in his eyes and was obviously deeply upset. "The police will be here soon to investigate, so it is probably best if you head back to Dhahran. I'll call you when we get ready to start up again. It will probably be tomorrow."

On the drive back to my office in Dhahran, I could think of nothing else but that little man from Yemen whose life had been abruptly ended so tragically that day. A little man who'd come to Saudi Arabia, like all the expatriate workers, to make the extra money so that he and his family back in the Yemen could have a better life. A family back in Yemen will now be without a breadwinner, and his children will be without a father. I never knew his name, but he always had a nod and smile for me as I walked by in the mornings.

Although safety is important at the Al-Qahtani plant where I had been working, the standards aren't up to a level that's found in Europe and North America. Whilst I worked at the Al-Qahtani plant, I was never given any safety training pertaining to the operation of day-to-day activity at the plant, or saw any training taking place.

There are many dangerous areas in the plant, where workers have to be very careful where they walk and what they do to prevent putting their life in jeopardy. These dangers were always on my mind when I walked around the plant.

The tragedy of this day would stick in my mind for a long time, and I would always think of that little Yemeni man when I passed the workstation where he lost his life so tragically that morning.

CHAPTER 14

The Beach

Aramco does its best to provide a variety of recreational facilities for people working in Saudi Arabia. In Dhahran there is a riding stable for people who like to ride horseback, two swimming pools, tennis courts, a golf club, a yacht club, a carpentry shop and the Aramco beach. The beach and yacht club are about a twenty-minute drive from Dhahran, and only open to Aramco employees and their families. The beach is equipped with barbecues. Picnic tables are covered with sunshade roofs as it gets too hot to sit for long in the sun.

Monica and I would sometimes take Blaine to the beach after I finished work when it was a little cooler. Ted and Linda Griffin and their two girls, Lorna and Annette, would sometimes join us for a barbecue supper. The soft sandy beach is ideal for children to play, and the water gets deep very gradually—safer for children who can't swim. The water is extremely salty on the Arabian Gulf which provides lots of buoyancy.

But due to the sandy bottom at the Aramco beach, it is not very clear with visibility at about ten to fifteen feet.

I joined the Aramco diving club which operates under the PADI system. Because the club didn't recognize some of the Canadian qualifications with NASDS, I had to recertify with PADI. In Canada, I had learned to share air with other divers using an octopus regulator. With PADI, I was required to use a single regulator to share air.

"I don't mind," I told Monica. "It is good practise and is for my own safety after all."

I practised in the Dhahran pool on Wednesday evening with my diving buddy Jim McColl from Vancouver. I met Jim on my first visit to the club, and we became friends and diving buddies from then on. We would often go to the beach together on a Thursday morning, and dive for an hour or until we ran out of air, just to keep in practice and for some exercise. There wasn't much to see at the local beaches as they all had sandy bottoms, and as a result didn't have a lot of marine life. I saw the odd sea snake, which are very poisonous. I found an article in the Dhahran library about them.

They can be 100cm or more in length. Bulky, but with a relatively small head. Yellow, sometimes pale dull green or grey, with dark bands along the length of the body. The top of the head is usually dark with a narrow yellow band forward of the small eyes. The undersides are pale and they have a flattened tail, typical of many sea snakes. This species is found throughout the Arabian region. Like all sea snakes, it is dangerous and a bite can be fatal. However, it is generally docile.

It is not uncommon to find a live sea snake washed ashore, or left stranded on the beach by a rapidly falling tide. Unable to move, they must wait for the high tide in order to return to their watery world. A sea snake lying motionless on a beach may appear dead, but it is wise to resist any temptation to handle such specimens, as they could well be alive. Although not aggressive, unwanted handling may provoke an attack. Sea snakes are the most venomous snakes in the world. One drop of sea snake venom is reputed to have the potency to kill five men. This high toxicity enables them to disable their cold-blooded prey, such as fish, crabs and squid on which they feed. Even young sea snakes that are born live at sea, have venom as potent as any adult. People are rarely bitten by sea snakes. Their apparently docile nature largely precludes the chance of a deliberate sea snake attack, and they're generally recognised as dangerous and avoided. The small mouth restricts their ability to bite any but the smallest appendage, such as a finger. The venom acting on a victim causes difficulty in breathing and swallowing, aching muscles and drooping eyelids.

Aramco has no record of anyone being bitten by a sea snake, according to the dive club instructors.

* * * * *

It was a hot June day when the Aramco Greyhound bus left Dhahran for a trip to Juraid Island.

There were twelve members of the Dhahran Dive Club and their families on board. The bus pulled out of Dhahran at 7:30 a.m., and was soon on the highway headed northwest to the port city of Jubail.

The island is in the Arabian Gulf, about two and a half hours by dhow from the port of Jubail. The dive club often rented a dhow and crew for the day for trips to Juraid Island. The dhow is a traditional wooden sailing vessel, many of which are now motorized. It is typically used in the Red Sea and Arabian Gulf for fishing and transportation of cargo.

"Juraid Island is not very well known," I told Jim. "Apparently it is little more than a sand bar surrounded by a coral reef."

The dive club had been there many times because the marine life is amazing. Jim McColl and I, and six other divers, were scheduled to do our deep dive certification.

Juraid Island is about 32 kilometres (20 miles) off the port city of Jubail. It is the southernmost tip of the chain of six coral-reef islands that exist where coral islands shouldn't exist. They support a unique ecosystem despite physical and chemical conditions that are normally considered to be too harsh. The six islands, south to north, are Juraid, Jana, Kurayn, Karan, Arabiya and Harqus. Karan is the largest at 1.3 square kilometres (half a square mile or 320 acres), and Harqus the smallest at 0.2 square kilometre (less than 50 acres).

I was reading this information to Jim from an Aramco magazine that I had brought along to read.

"Apparently there are a lot of mice on the islands, probably introduced to the islands as stowaways from passing boats. Don't bring home any unwanted passengers in your picnic basket."

"The town of Al-Jubail has ancient roots," I continued. "Human habitation dates back at least 7,000 years, when the people of Dilmun, whose civilization radiated up and down the Persian Gulf, established a settlement there. It has a fine natural harbour, with an abundance of fish and pearl oysters."

It took about one-and-a-half hours to cover the 65 miles to Jubail. The security guards on the port gate were aware that our group was coming, and after a head count the bus was given clearance to enter the port.

The Arab fishing dhow that was rented by the dive club was waiting for us at the dock, along with its captain and two deck hands. The diving and swimming equipment was quickly offloaded from the underside storage of the bus, and stowed on the deck of the dhow. A head count was taken by the dive club instructors as everyone climbed on board, and made themselves comfortable as best they could on the deck surface for the trip to the island. There were no creature comforts on this dhow, as it was a working fishing boat of about fifteen metres in length, with a single mast and small central wheelhouse. It had a distinctive profile, high at the stern and sweeping low towards the bow, before rising to a characteristically jutting prow. The most common type of dhow in the Gulf is the *shu'ai,* which can fairly be described as the workhorse of the inshore waters, performing in both fishing and coastal trading roles.

The deckhands, dressed in traditional white thobes, cast off the bow and stern lines. With a gentle push we moved away from the dock; the captain fired up the engine and we were underway heading out of the harbour.

Jubail harbour is quite large with a vast array of vessels in port, from small fishing dhows to large ocean-going freighters unloading their cargo from around the world. A big portion of Aramco's supplies for the oil installations comes into the Port of Jubail.

We chugged out of the harbour and headed for the open sea. I noticed a number of cockroaches climbing up the wall of the wheelhouse adjacent to where I was sitting on the deck. I pointed them out to Jim, who screwed up his face in disgust.

"Keep them away from me," he said. "I hate the things."

It was going to be another hot day, and there was little shade on deck where we could get out of the hot sun. As advised, we'd brought along lots of water, and it was going to be needed in order to stay hydrated. Seagulls flew alongside the dhow, probably in hopes of a handout from the passengers which they occasionally got.

The sea was calm with hardly a ripple, and not even a hint of a cooling breeze.

It was going to be a long hot trip, I thought.

I chatted to Jim, my dive buddy, about numerous topics to while away the time.

Juraid Island has very little elevation, maybe two or three metres, so it is difficult to see from a distance. It was almost two-and-a-half hours' travel time from the port to the island. The island was just a slither of sand sticking out of the water and hardly visible until we were actually there.

The captain anchored the dhow alongside the coral reef that surrounds the island. He advised everyone in broken English that we should all be on board at three o' clock for the trip back to Jubail. The sun was high in the sky now, and it was shaping up to be another very hot day. A ladder was attached to the side of the dhow to allow everyone to get in and out of the water. A number of people dove off the deck to cool down a little before donning their snorkel equipment. The water temperature was a warm 85 degrees Fahrenheit, which seemed like bath water.

I and five other dive club members, who were scheduled to do deep dive certification, wasted no time in putting on our equipment. After a briefing from our instructor, we were soon in the water swimming away from the dhow for our descent. The instructor gave the signal and we started to make our way to a planned depth of about eighty feet. The water was very clear, with a visibility of forty to sixty feet. My usual diving buddy, my friend from Vancouver Jim McColl, was my diving buddy for this dive.

When we were at fifty feet, Jim signalled that he was ascending. When we got to the surface, Jim said he was having problems equalizing the pressure in his ears. After a few minutes the instructor and the other divers also surfaced, as they were wondering why Jim and I had ascended. The instructor said we would try again, and advised Jim to go slow on his descent and equalize his ears frequently.

Jim managed to get to about sixty feet on the second attempt, but could go no deeper due to discomfort in his ears and had to surface. All the other divers surfaced with us. The instructor said we would make one more attempt, and if Jim couldn't get to the planned depth, we would abort the dive. The instructor advised Jim to be very careful not to exceed his comfort level, which could result in damage to his eardrums. At the third attempt Jim could only manage to get to forty feet before he was forced to surface.

After the other divers surfaced, the diving instructor asked us if we saw the shark. Three divers saw it circling, but Jim and I didn't see it, probably because we were concentrating on our attempt to descend.

"The shark circled right around you, Mark," the instructor said. "I'm surprised you didn't see it."

"No, I didn't see a thing," I replied.

We'd drifted away from the dhow, having been caught in a slight current. No one had noticed we were drifting, as we were so intent on trying to do our deep dive. The dhow appeared to be about eight hundred yards from where we were now located.

"We'll have to do a surface swim back to the dhow," the instructor said. "We'll not be able to stop for a rest or we'll continually lose ground."

It was a long swim back, which I completed by alternating strokes on my back and stomach. All the way back I couldn't take my mind off the shark that visited us.

I kept wondering if at any moment I would have a chunk taken out of my leg or worse. At least the splashing from the swimmers would help to keep the shark away.

When I finally reached the safety of the dhow, I was exhausted from the swim. I clung to the ladder on the side of the dhow, until all the other divers were onboard, before climbing the ladder and flopping on the deck like a wet rag. I sat there in silence for a while contemplating the swim, and the shark that I didn't see. I wondered how things would have turned out if the shark would have attacked one of us. Not a pleasant thought being so far away from medical help, and a two-and-a-half-hour slow trip back to port.

"I'm surprised you didn't see the shark," the instructor said to me. "It circled you and Jim quite closely before swimming away. It was about ten to twelve feet in length and was probably a tiger shark, as they come in to the island after the turtles that nest there. When I get back to Dhahran, I'll talk to one of Aramco's marine biologists and see what type of shark he thinks it was."

"Did you see the shark, Jim?" I asked.

"No I didn't," Jim replied. "I think I'm glad I didn't."

"Likewise," I replied.

We sat on the deck eating lunch and watching the other people snorkelling on the inner side of the coral reef. The sun shone down relentlessly from a hazy ball, and there was little in the way of shade on the deck of the dhow. After lunch we relaxed for a while before taking the short swim to the island. The island wasn't anything more than a sand bar with a few tufts of grass growing haphazardly in the undulating surface. The island's elevation was little more than a metre or two, and we were able to walk around most of the island in very short order.

Not a very exciting place, I thought.

No reason to see it except for the coral reef and the abundance of tropical fish that inhabited its jagged, crusty walls.

Jim and I sat on the beach until the captain of the dhow gave the signal for everyone to board for the return trip to Jubail.

It seemed like a long trip back to port, but everyone was thankful for a cool breeze that was cresting the deck. Aided by the gentle rocking of the dhow I drifted off to sleep. It was cooling a little by the time we entered the port of Jubail, and tied up alongside the dock where our bus was waiting.

We quickly disembarked and loaded our equipment back into the lower storage of the bus. All the tired passengers climbed aboard the bus which felt like an oven inside. The diesel engine came to life, and within a few minutes we were in the air-conditioned comfort of the Greyhound heading for the port gate. The bus came to a gentle stop at the gate and an armed security guard climbed aboard for a head count. The driver signed a paper on the guard's clipboard, and we were waved out of the gate for our journey home.

The trip home was uneventful, except for a large Mercedes that passed us on our side of the divided highway, going in the opposite direction to the bus. The bus driver yelled out, "look at this idiot." The Mercedes sped by; the driver apparently oblivious to the fact that he was on the wrong side of the divided highway.

A few days after we returned home, the diving instructor contacted me and informed me that he had spoken with the marine biologist. He confirmed that the shark we saw was most probably a tiger shark, which are normally eight to twelve feet in length.

"I'm glad he wasn't hungry," I replied. "I wasn't ready to be fish bait or to be his lunchtime snack."

"Its name is derived from the dark stripes down its body that are similar to a tiger pattern. The stripes fade as the shark matures," he informed me. "Its usual diet consists of fish, seals, birds, smaller sharks, squid, turtles, dolphins and sometimes humans—just kidding. The tiger shark has a very aggressive nature, and is second only to the great white shark in the number of attacks on humans. They're considered to be one of the most dangerous of sharks."

"That's nice to know," I replied. "I'll be sure to keep out of their way in future."

When I put the phone down, a cold shiver went up my spine as I contemplated what could have resulted in a very serious accident at Juraid Island, had the shark attacked one of the divers in that remote location. Jim and I returned to Juraid Island a month later, and again a year later on diving trips, but didn't see any sharks on either occasion.

CHAPTER 15

Blood and Alcohol

Austin Barton walked into my office one day and sat down on the chair by my desk.

"How's it going Mark?" he asked. "How are things at Al-Qahtani?"

"Good," I replied. "Al-Qahtani is very busy at present because the pipeline groups have been coating a lot of thirty-inch pipe during the past month."

"Your supervisor Dave Hansen is going back to the United Kingdom next week on three weeks repat," Austin advised me. "I'll be sitting in for him as supervisor of the Vendor Inspection Division while he is away, so any problems come and see me."

"You bet," I replied. "How is your video tape club going? Did you get the parking problem outside your house resolved?"

"Sure did," Austin replied, "I split the club up into three pieces and sold three shares for twelve thousand dollars each. Now the parking problem has disappeared and Aramco is happy. Also, I receive a royalty of fifty cents on each tape that's rented out from the three shareholders. I still supply nine new movie tapes a month to the shareholders, so the club will continue to expand. It has turned out to be a nice little money spinner."

"You must have time on your hands now! What are you going to do to occupy your spare time?"

"I've some ideas," Austin replied, "which could turn out to be quite lucrative. I'm working on it, so we'll see how it pans out."

Austin is quite the entrepreneur, I thought, as Austin left my office to refill his coffee cup.

Jim DeAngelo was on the phone during my conversation with Austin. He put down the phone and said to me, "I overheard part of your conversation with Austin. He is going to get himself into a lot of hot water with Aramco if he doesn't watch out. He seems to spend a lot of his working time on private matters which will eventually catch up with him if he is not careful."

"I agree! Aramco won't put up with that if they find out."

"Do you give blood at the hospital?" Jim asked. "They're always looking for donors, and they pay quite well. I think the current rate is about three hundred and fifty riyals. I'm scheduled to go this afternoon and give if my blood count is OK."

"No, I've never given blood," I replied. "What do you have to do to be a donor?"

"Just phone this number."

Jim jotted down the number on a yellow Post-it Note and handed it to me.

"They'll make an appointment for you, and after you've given once, they put you on a recall list as a regular donor."

"Thanks Jim," I replied. "I'll call them now and see if I can get an appointment."

A few minutes later I was talking to the blood bank. After asking me a few questions, they gave me an appointment for the following Monday at 8:30 a.m.

"What's your blood type?" Jim asked.

"I really can't remember," I replied. "I'll have to check when I get home."

"They'll find out very quickly," Jim said. "If it is similar to a lot of Saudis, you'll probably get called quite often."

The following Monday just before 8:30 a.m. I entered the blood bank office at the Dhahran hospital. I was ushered to a room where a number of people were lying on beds giving blood. This was all new to me because I had never given blood before. I was always so busy back home in Canada that it never occurred to me to give blood when the Red Cross, on their occasional radio announcements, called for donors. I don't like having needles stuck in my arm, which was another reason why I hadn't given blood before.

That's a bit childish and selfish, and just a feeble excuse for not making the effort to help a good cause, I thought.

A nurse, whose name was Lynn according to the badge on her white lab coat, asked me to sit on a bed. She handed me a clipboard with a form attached, and asked me to complete it.

"Our primary concern is that giving blood won't affect your health in any way. We also have to make sure your blood is safe for patients. We just need to find out whether or not you can give blood. Some medical conditions, even colds, can all affect your suitability, although usually it's just temporary. We need your co-operation in answering these questions. And, of course, all your details will be treated in the strictest confidence. I'll be back in a few minutes," she said.

I went through the list of questions checking them off appropriately. Are you pregnant?

Don't think so, I thought.

Have you had your ears pierced during the past year? Have you had Hepatitis B or C? Have you ever been given money or drugs for sex? Have you ever received blood? The list went on and on. Finally I reached the end and signed and dated it.

They're very thorough, I thought, *but I'm sure they have to be extremely careful.*

Lynn came back and collected the clipboard and form from me.

"What's your blood type?" she asked me.

"B positive," I replied.

"We'll check it anyway," she said.

"You'll probably be called upon to give blood often as most Saudis are B positive. Put your legs up on the bed, Mark, and we'll get you hooked up and started."

I turned away when the needle was inserted in my arm. I don't like watching a needle being poked into my arm, but was comfortable with it after it was done.

"You don't like watching the needle do you?" Lynn said.

"You noticed. I think I would pass out if I watched it," I replied. "I can't even watch it being done on TV; it makes me feel really funny."

After I gave blood, I was given a cup of tea and a cookie, and advised to relax for twenty minutes before getting up. Lynn advised me to check at the front desk on the way out, where I would be paid for my blood donation. Twenty minutes later I collected three hundred and fifty riyals. This was the first of many donations I would make. I received frequent calls to donate from the blood bank. Sometimes my blood cell count was too low to make a donation, and I would be advised to come back in a month or two.

* * * * *

It was a Wednesday morning in late September, just prior to an early morning office meeting, that I heard the latest news that was spreading around Dhahran.

Apparently a high-ranking long-term 49-year-old division manager in the drilling department was caught with a still by the local police. He was arrested and thrown in jail. It happened at about six thirty in the morning, just when Aramco employees were starting to go to work for the day. Someone from the office had seen the Saudi police breaking up a still with a sledgehammer on the front lawn of a big home in Dhahran. They were making an exhibition of it as an example to other expats: don't get involved with the making and selling of illegal alcohol! The timing was appropriate. The police knew a number of people would see them at that time of the morning as they were making their way to work. The news was spreading like a wildfire around the camp, and it would be just a matter of time before everyone found out who was involved.

"He's probably now wishing he'd never seen a still," Jim exclaimed. "I can't understand these people that do this, especially when they have really good paying jobs with Aramco. They must need their heads examined. He will probably not get out of jail for a long time, after the judicial system gets through with him."

Later that day rumour had it that the manager involved had been with Aramco for 18 years, and was due to retire in December and return to the United States.

"I can't understand getting involved with making illegal alcohol," Monica said, when I told her about it over supper that evening. "Why are some people here so greedy? I have difficulty understanding their motivation when they're in a high-paying job with lots of benefits. Now that man will spend a few years in jail, and pay a high fine for his greed. What an idiot!"

"What's an idiot?" asked Blaine, who'd obviously been listening to his mother's comments. He was often picking up on new words he overheard.

"Well, it is someone who's unable to learn," she replied, hoping this simplified answer would satisfy his curiosity. Monica sensed that he had accepted this answer, but knew he was storing this new word for future use.

It became the topic of conversation around camp for the next week, but as no further news became available, it was temporally forgotten.

We later learned that he was taken before a judge who told him he was guilty of operating a still, and he was sentenced to two years imprisonment, and 200 lashes, to be given in increments of 50.

It was mid-December when further information started working its way around Dhahran, about the high-ranking drilling department manager who'd been thrown in jail for running a still. By this time his name was known, and most people were aware that his family had been sent back to the United States after his incarceration. Jim advised me when he arrived at the office on Sunday morning about the latest story that was circulating. Apparently three Saudi police had escorted a man fitting the description of the Drilling Department manager to the Dhahran airport late on Friday evening. He had been seen in the boarding area with the three armed guards, and was in handcuffs and leg shackles. When the Saudia Airlines flight was ready for boarding, he was escorted onto the plane. Just before the cabin door was closed, his handcuffs and leg shackles were removed and the aircraft departed for its destination, which was believed to be Frankfurt, Germany. He had served five months of his prison term, and didn't receive any of the lashes.

"I think he must have been supplying someone high-up with Sid," Jim said, "and they arranged for his deportation back to the States. Perhaps it was a high-up Saudi official, or someone high up within the Aramco administration. Either that or somehow he was able to bribe someone and get his release. Or, perhaps he had something on someone high-up and used it to get his release. I'm sure we'll probably never find out what happened. All I can say is that he was extremely lucky he didn't have to spend several years in that Saudi prison in Al-Khobar."

"That's one that got away with it," I replied.

"That doesn't happen often," Jim said. "It's just not worth it. Think of all the grief he caused his family for the sake of a few extra dollars."

CHAPTER 16

Monica Starts Work

Six months after Monica and I moved into temporary housing in Dhahran, Monica went to see the head of physiotherapy at the Dhahran hospital. Aramco wouldn't offer her a job when we went through orientation in Houston. Because she has a degree in physiotherapy, they advised her to apply at the Dhahran hospital after she arrived in Saudi Arabia. As Blaine was only two and a half years old, she decided that she would like to work if they would take her on a part-time basis. There were several people on camp who were operating daycares for children. Blaine would go to a daycare for the hours that she would be working.

"We've a job in the physio department," John Calmar (head of the physiotherapy department) advised Monica. "The hours are flexible if you would like to work on a part-time basis, but you would have to work a minimum of six hours a day."

"That would be fine," Monica replied. "Could I start at eight and finish at two thirty with a half hour for lunch?"

"That would be ideal," John replied. "When would you like to start?"

"I could start next week if that would be OK. It will give me a few days to arrange a daycare for my son, Blaine."

John took Monica on a tour of the department that seemed to be well equipped. From what she could see, there appeared to be four other physiotherapists working in the department that day.

"My secretary, Sandra, will help you complete the paperwork, and we'll look forward to seeing you on Saturday," John said, as he escorted her to the secretary's office.

Monica was looking forward to starting work. It would give her a change of routine, and a chance to meet some more people and make new friends. The extra money would also help. We would probably be able to save all of my salary when she was working.

Monica had decided she would leave Blaine with a friend, Danielle Fenton, who had two boys, Garth Junior and James, and was running a daycare.

However, Monica wanted to find a secondary daycare for Blaine for when Danielle was away on repat. She remembered that Jamie Baynes, who'd lived next to us in Sea View and was in temporary housing on camp, was also running a daycare.

It was a very hot day again, which was usual for the time of year. Monica had wrapped a cloth over Blaine's pushchair to protect his arms from the steel framework. His little arms would have received a burn if he were to touch the frame. After collecting the mail from the post office box, they walked over to the snack bar by the swimming pool and library. Monica stopped to get an ice-cream cone to share with Blaine. It was refreshing, and helped to cool them both down a little before the walk home. The well air-conditioned snack bar also helped.

As Jamie's home was only a short walk from our home, and it was only 2:30 p.m., Monica decided to walk the extra distance and visit Jamie. The tree-lined streets and alleyways provided some respite from the relentless heat of the sun. Some of the trees had huge overhangs and provided lots of shade. Others, like the date palms that stood tall and straight, perhaps twenty feet high, provided little shade.

They made their way through the older part of Dhahran where most of the homes were side-by-side bungalows. Some of the homes were surrounded with high walls or tall shrubbery hedges for privacy. Many Saudi workers and their families now lived on camp, and privacy for them was a priority. Occasionally, Monica would catch the glimpse of a pool through the edge of an entrance gate or gap in a hedge. Some of the long-time residences had these extra luxuries which had been at individual expense. These homes rarely came up for bid on the housing list, and if they did, most went to employees with lots of housing points. The more housing points an employee accumulated, the better the home they could acquire.

Halfway up a steep incline in the road, Monica stopped for a rest beneath the shade of a large palm tree. She noticed that she was only a short distance from the daycare, and could hear the sound of children as they played in the garden. Blaine had been lulled to sleep with the gentle jogging of the pushchair. As they approached and unlatched the tall wooden gate to the garden, a bell sounded and a dog started barking, giving warning of their approach. The garden was surrounded by a chain-link fence which was almost completely covered with a pink flowering shrub on the sidewalk side of the bungalow. Four little boys and a girl were happily playing with toys under a sunshade in the large grass-covered garden. A tall overweight lady in a long flowing caftan-style cotton dress greeted Monica with a welcoming smile.

"Can I help you," she enquired, as Monica made her way to the door.

"I'm looking for a second daycare for my son," Monica said. "I was advised by a friend that you were running a daycare"

"Welcome," she said as she extended her hand to Monica. "I remember you from Sea View."

"Yes, we were next door to you in Sea View."

"Please come in, Monica. You're just in time for juice and cookies that I've made for the children."

Monica could smell the aroma of the freshly baked cookies which Jamie had placed on a large plate on the kitchen countertop. Jamie explained that her husband, Evan, worked in the Inspection Department doing non-destructive testing, and was away on field trips quite frequently.

"I run the daycare for something to keep me busy," she said. "Also, it gives us a little spending money when we go on vacation, and it provides some friends for Shane, my little three-year-old, to play with. She's the only child at home."

"My husband works in the Inspection Department," Monica said. "I wonder if he knows Evan"

"Isn't that a coincidence," Jamie exclaimed. "It is a small world."

They chatted for a while and Monica thought that Blaine would enjoy being there with Jamie and the children. Jamie was someone she would feel comfortable leaving Blaine with. When Blaine woke up, Jamie gave him juice and a cookie, and called the other children in for their snack. After Monica had made arrangements for Blaine's secondary daycare, Blaine played with the other children for a while. He seemed to get along well with them, playing happily in the garden.

When they departed for the walk home, Monica noticed the bell affixed to the top of the gate. If the gate was opened by the children Jamie would hear the bell ring.

That's a good idea, she thought, *I think Blaine will be safe here.*

That evening over supper Monica related her day to me.

"I don't know Evan," I said, "but will make some enquiries the next time I'm in the office. That sounds like a very good place for Blaine to stay when Danielle Fenton is away. Having some other little children to play with will be something he will look forward to, I'm sure."

I noticed the little gecko that had taken up residence in our house. It scurried up the wall and onto the ceiling.

"Look Blaine," I said, as I pointed it out to him. The gecko was about two to three inches long, and light brown in colour, and had been in the house for about a month, I estimated. "I think he is your friend, Blaine."

"You'll probably see him in your bedroom from time to time."

I didn't want him to be alarmed at seeing the small reptile, especially if it were to find its way into his bedroom.

"He won't come near you, Blaine. They like to crawl along the ceiling and catch little flies."

"What do they do with the flies?" Blaine asked.

"They eat them," I replied. "That's what they eat for supper."

Monica's first week at work was interesting. The work was essentially the same as that in North America but the patients were of many different nationalities. Most spoke good English, but her knowledge of Arabic that she'd been studying at evening classes would definitely be an asset. Because Saudi women aren't allowed to drive a motor vehicle, the husband has to take the wife and children to appointments. This can result in a lot of time off work for the husband, especially if he has more than one wife.

Many of the Saudi women wear the abaya, also referred to as a burqa or jilbab, a veil that Muslim woman wear on top of regular clothing as part of their Islamic clothing attire. The primary purpose of wearing the abaya or jilbab is to cover the Muslim woman as instructed in the Islamic religion. Sometimes the face is exposed; sometimes it is covered. As a result, Saudi women have to be treated by a female therapist.

One of the first things Monica noticed in the department washroom was a pictorial notice giving instruction on how to use the toilet. The instruction indicates that the toilet has to be sat on, rather than stood on like the old traditional middle-eastern facility.

Monica will always remember the new Saudi patient who came to the clinic with a back problem. He wore a typical white Saudi thobe, a red and white checked ghutra and igal.

A thobe is a loose, long-sleeved, ankle-length garment. Summer thobes are white and made of cotton, and winter thobes can be darker and made of wool. The ghutra is a square scarf, made of cotton or silk, folded in a triangle and worn over the tagiyah, or skullcap. It is often all white, or red and white checked. There is no significance placed on which kind the man wears. The igal is the black rope-like cord used to secure the ghutra in place. (My American workmates called the igal a fan belt.) The patient said he needed a specific size back support as a replacement for the one he had.

"I'll check to see if we've one your size," she advised him.

He was a man of average build but a little overweight for his height. When she returned she said, "I'm sorry. We don't seem to have one in your size."

He glared at her in disgust and said, "Women don't know anything, let me speak to your supervisor."

Monica was furious at his derogatory comment, but restrained herself from making a sarcastic reply that he would have deserved.

"Please wait, I'll get my supervisor," she said.

Monica quickly found John Calmar, the department head, and explained the situation to him.

"Don't worry about it, Monica," he replied. "I'll speak to him."

John was from Helena, Montana, and was a quiet-spoken man with a lot of patience. He had been in Saudi Arabia for a number of years, and there was little he hadn't come across during his tenure. Monica watched as he spoke to the man, who accepted his response without question. After the man had left, John said, "Don't let it get to you, Monica. He is not your typical polite Saudi."

Monica's blood was still boiling, but a quick cup of coffee before her next patient was all that it took to settle her down.

Pat Miller, her next patient, was a young petroleum engineer, originally from Humboldt, Saskatchewan. Pat had been to see her a few times before with a shoulder problem—as a result of an old injury from playing ice hockey. He was a good-natured man who didn't seem to take life too seriously. He was always ready with a funny comment or joke, or had a funny story to tell.

"How are you today, Monica?" he asked, as he sat on the treatment table and removed his shirt for treatment.

"I'm OK," she replied with a grin. "I've had better days, I suppose."

As Monica treated his shoulder, she related her experience with the previous patient.

"Well he was right, wasn't he," Pat replied. "Women don't know anything," he teased.

"You better be careful what you say, Pat," she quipped, "or you'll go home with a worse shoulder than what you came in with." She laughed.

She wouldn't have said that if she didn't think he could take a joke.

Pat and his wife, Colette, would eventually become good friends of Monica and me. We all came from the same city in Canada prior to joining Aramco, and both had young children. It gave us a lot in common.

Monica met lots of people through her work in the hospital. Monica and I attended many of the social functions that the physio department organized from time to time. It resulted in a number of new friendships. We also met several people with young children as a result of Blaine's daycare. It led to a group of five little boys about the same age as Blaine who were all born in the month of August. They later became known as the August boys, and would all celebrate their birthdays together.

Monica could relate many interesting stories about work in the Dhahran physiotherapy department.

One day, a Saudi lady came in and handed her appointment slip to the receptionist. When the receptionist checked in the appointment book, there appeared to be no appointment listed for her. However, the date on the appointment slip was for the correct day. Then she noticed the year. The Saudi lady was exactly a year late.

CHAPTER 17

Drugs and Alcohol

I was still working at the pipe coating yard in Dammam, overseeing the operation on behalf of Aramco and protecting their interest. I had made a number of changes to the Aramco standards and specifications for the coating operations at this facility, bringing them in line with how the work was done. Over the years, the pipe coating plant had made changes to the coating processes, but the changes were never recorded in the Aramco coating standards.

I ran into a lot of opposition from some of the employees at the facility in doing this, including the general manager. They thought I was trying to find fault with their work, but that wasn't my intent at all.

Finally I called a meeting with their general manager and quality manager, and sat down with them to explain what I was trying to achieve. I showed them that some parts of their operation were in contravention of Aramco specifications, due to things that had changed over the years. Eventually, they were convinced I was trying to help them rather than make problems, and as a result earned their respect. Subsequently, I rewrote the Aramco standards for the pipe coating processes, under the guidance and review of the Aramco Material Selection Division, which took several months to complete.

Al-Qahtani employed about thirty people in their coating facility on the south side of Dammam. They'd expanded operations to a second facility on the north side of the city which primarily catered for the internal coating of pipe. I oversaw both operations, and had a full time Korean servorg inspector working for me at the new facility.

Al-Qahtani had two quality managers, one that was responsible for the day-to-day quality assurance, James Henderson, and a laboratory manager Garth Rhymer. Both men were hired from the United Kingdom, and lived in a housing compound that was owned by Al-Qahtani in the suburbs of Dammam.

Garth had two children, a five-year-old boy and a seven-year-old girl. His wife, Bettie, and their children were living with Garth in a small villa on the Al-Qahtani housing compound.

Garth was a quiet-spoken man about 32 years of age with fair curly hair and moustache, and he wore rimless glasses. He was rarely seen in the pipe coating yard, as his job involved laboratory analysis of coating materials and product samples taken during coating operations. Most often, he could be seen through the glass-fronted laboratory wearing a white lab coat and peering through a microscope at slides and material samples. He would be meticulously recording all the data in a log for future reference in case a problem developed in service on any of the pipe that Al-Qahtani coated for Aramco.

By British standards, he was well paid for being in a foreign country. He received free housing, a cost of living increase to compensate for the additional cost in Saudi Arabia, return airfare to the United Kingdom once a year for himself and his family, and a substantial salary increase for foreign service. Bettie, his wife, looked after two other children for a friend during working hours which gave her a few extra riyals spending money.

Bettie, like a lot of women, found Saudi Arabia very restrictive. This resulted in the need to get out of the kingdom a little more often than once a year. Bettie and her friend, Karley, had been looking at holiday brochures from a local travel agent and were planning a short five-day vacation in Thailand.

"We can fly Kuwait Airways out of Bahrain," Karley said. "With one stop in Kuwait city, it takes about 13 hours to Bangkok."

The two girls had been planning this trip for some time and now it was looking like reality.

"Should be fun," Bettie said. "Especially without the men. I hear Thailand is very free, and custom-made clothing is very cheap compared to the United Kingdom."

Neither woman was into drugs, but prior to leaving the United Kingdom both had smoked a little marijuana, which wasn't legally available in Saudi Arabia.

"Will be nice to have a few drinks and maybe a little weed," Karley said. "It has been a long time since I had a good time."

"It really will," Bettie said. "Garth gets the odd bottle of gin, and we get Sid from time to time, but other than that we only have soft drinks. I'm not that keen on Sid, but Garth seems to like it when he can't get anything else."

* * * * *

Many social structures in Thailand share some resemblance to the United Kingdom. Thailand has a history of scholarly links to Britain. Many members of the Thai royalty have received schooling in England.

Similar laws exist in Thailand to that of Britain, especially policy on drug suppression and system of law. However, the enforcement and penalties used by the two nations are very different.

The most noticeable difference in drug laws between the two nations is the death penalty in Thailand for trafficking and possession of dangerous drugs, such as heroin.

Rehabilitation counselling is available, and is also mandatory in Thailand for all forms of drug use, including marijuana. In the United Kingdom, the maximum penalty is life imprisonment. This is usually for dealing in strong drugs with intent to supply.

Basically the legal framework is very similar. However, in a practical sense things are very different. Thailand's police have faced accusations of abuse of power, similar to that of Mexico. Stories exist that drugs confiscated by police have a strong chance of being re-sold by the police. Many police forces around the world are corrupt in some form or another so it is not unreasonable in suggesting it is true.

Due to the proximity of Thailand to the Golden Triangle and to ethnic resistance groups that traffic in drugs for funding for weapons, drug trafficking in and around Thailand is commonplace. The availability and use of drugs is far greater than that of the United Kingdom but raids are frequent and punishment swift.

Calls for more control, accountability and reform of the police are frequent but have always been resisted.

Be aware that if you think Thailand is lax in its drug enforcement, and is an easy and cheap place to get and use drugs, think again. Drug laws are strict, penalties high, and no allowance is made for foreigners.

When Bettie and Karley arrived in Bangkok they were tired from their long flight, and had seen enough of airports for one day.

In the Thai language, Bangkok means "City of Angels." It was once a small trading post at the mouth of the Chao Phraya River, and became Thailand's capital city in 1768. With a population today of approximately five million people spread over an area of about 1,500 square kilometres, Bangkok has 900,000 registered motor vehicles. Due to the number of canals and waterways that divide the city into separate patches of land, Bangkok is known as the "Venice of the East."

The women had made a reservation at the Grace Hotel on Sukhumvit Road. The room rate was good, and as they didn't plan to spend much time in the hotel, they couldn't justify paying a lot of money for a place to sleep. What they didn't know was that the Grace is in the centre of the red-light district, and only became aware of this when they talked to Dave, a fellow passenger on their flight over.

"The Grace and Nana hotels were once the R and R hotels for the American forces during the Vietnam war," Dave said. "The American soldiers were allowed to take girls to their rooms. The police turned a blind eye to it then; a tradition that hasn't changed even today for these two hotels," Dave advised them. "The Grace was primarily for the officers, and the Nana for the combat troops. There is nothing wrong with the hotels as long as you don't mind the many prostitutes that frequent the lobby, restaurant and bar. The rooms are clean, and the room rates are very good compared to other hotels. I've stayed in both hotels with my wife several times," Dave said. "We've never had a problem."

Collecting their baggage and clearing customs had seemed to take forever due to the volume of people being processed. After the long wait at baggage claims, they made their way to the airport exit and the lineup of waiting taxis. At the exit they immediately noticed the high humidity.

"The taxi air-conditioning doesn't seem to be working very well," Karley remarked. "I'll be glad to get to the hotel and get a shower."

They were a little overwhelmed by the congestion, city noise and air pollution from the traffic. It wasn't anything like the pictures they'd seen in the glossy magazine from the travel agent. There seemed to be people and traffic everywhere, and a predominance of the little three wheeled tuk-tuk taxis in the downtown area.

"Got to ride in one of those," Bettie remarked.

At least once anyway, a friend had told them.

As Dave had said, the Grace hotel was clean, but there were often a lot of skimpily clad girls around, particularly in the evening hours. It didn't bother Bettie and Karley as they only passed through the lobby on their way in or out, and the call girls were only interested in the single men.

During their short holiday, the women did some of the touristy things like visiting a few of the many exotic temples and the floating markets. They took a tour along the Chao Praya River in one of the colourfully painted longtail boats and rode the tuk-tuks to some of the major tourist attractions. They each had custom blouses and skirts made, and shopped for brightly coloured hand-woven Thai silk scarves at some of the many boutique stores as they wandered around. They each bought crocodile skin belts and wallets as gifts for their husbands, which they found very cheap in the markets, and silk Kimono dressing gowns for the children.

They ate at interesting restaurants, and visited some of the many jazz clubs, ultra-cool bars and trendy clubs. They relaxed with an enjoyable cocktail which they couldn't do in Saudi Arabia.

It all came to an end too quickly, and they were on their way home again on a Kuwait Airlines flight. They were tired when they arrived back in Bahrain and boarded the final flight to Dhahran. That flight is reputed to be the shortest flight in the world, about 30 miles. The aircraft barely gets airborne and then has to land again.

It was starting to get dusk as their last flight touched down on the tarmac of Dhahran airport. The sky was a hazy red and gold, as the last traces of the fireball looking sun sank below the horizon.

"That was a great little holiday," Bettie said. "Did you enjoy it, Karley?"

"Yes I did," replied Karley. "We'll have to do something like that again but to a different location."

"That would be fun, I'd like that." Bettie said.

The aircraft came to a halt, and passengers were starting to unfasten their seatbelts and retrieve their carry-on bags from the overhead bins.

At Dhahran airport there are no terminal ramps. All aircraft park a short distance from the terminal and passengers use stairs to exit the aircraft.

Karley was in an aisle seat and had retrieved her carry-on bag. Bettie had a small carry-on that was placed beneath the seat. She followed her friend to the aircraft door and they started down the stairs. It was a warm evening, with a slight cooling breeze coming inland off the ocean. As soon as Bettie's feet touched the tarmac, three uniformed police appeared to come out of nowhere. Two of them grabbed Bettie's arms and one grabbed her small bag, as they whisked her away to a waiting vehicle. Karley had turned around to look for her friend just in time to see her being escorted away.

"Bettie," she yelled. "What's going on?"

One of the police officers said, "Go, go" and pointed her away with a wave of his hand as Bettie was quickly bundled into their vehicle and driven away.

Karley was devastated, and began to shake. She didn't remember walking the one hundred yards to the terminal building. All kinds of things were racing through her mind. She couldn't believe what had just happened to her friend. Her only thought now was to get through the terminal, and hopefully find Bettie's husband Garth, who'd arranged to meet them at the airport. She was starting to sweat profusely, and knew that she had to take control of herself before going through the airport security with her bags.

Karley had been through Dhahran airport a number of times and was very familiar with the security check. As she was waiting for her checked luggage to arrive, her thoughts were with her friend and how the police were treating her. Bettie had purchased a small quantity of marijuana from a man in one of the bars they'd visited in Bangkok. A second delivery that she planned to take home was made to their hotel. Karley had warned her friend about not taking it back. Bettie was confident she could get it into Saudi Arabia without any problem. The delivery, which was made to the hotel, was a little problematic. She had an argument over the cost which had turned out to be higher than agreed. Eventually, she talked the man down and he left a little disgruntled.

After retrieving her bag, Karley headed for the customs desk. The nervous tension in her body was starting to settle down. She'd stopped shaking but was still bathed in perspiration. She mopped her face with a tissue and followed the other passengers to the customs area where her bags would be checked.

Karley would never get used to the madhouse of this check. It was a free-for-all of people pushing towards a counter where your bag would be opened and searched. There was no exception. All bags were opened, and often the contents partly or completely removed, depending on the mood of the customs officer. At the very least, hands would grope through the contents and drag out anything that felt suspicious. Carefully packed bags could wind up in a mess of clothing and personal articles being casually discarded into the lid of the case or onto the counter.

When the officer was satisfied that Karley wasn't bringing in any contraband goods, he marked the outside of the case with a white chalk and she was free to repack her case. She had several bags, so from experience on previous trips had decided to pay a porter to help her through customs. The porter was especially useful on this trip. She was on her own, and he was accustomed to this madhouse and could expedite the check process as they pushed their way to the counter. All of Karley's bags were checked, and after repacking the clothing that the customs officer had pulled out, she headed towards the exit. A security officer at the door checked her bags for the chalk mark, and she was free to exit the building.

Outside the exit of the customs hall at the meeting area, the railings were lined with people waiting for friends, relatives or business associates to arrive. A number of notices were being held up displaying the name of the person they were meeting. This was typical when business people are being met for the first time.

Karley quickly found Garth, whose first words were, "Where's Bettie?"

"Tell you outside, Garth," Karley replied, as Garth grabbed her suitcase and they made for the exit.

Once outside, Karley was stricken with emotion as she tearfully related to Garth what had happened.

"She had marijuana taped to her waist. I told her not to do it but she didn't listen."

Garth was devastated by the news but knew that it was pointless to try and find his wife, or get any news of her from the police. She would probably have been taken from the airport to either the Al-Khobar or

Dammam police stations. He would have to get the company lawyer involved in the morning to get any news of her predicament.

Bettie was sentenced to five years in jail. She was sent to a jail outside of Jeddah.

The Saudis take a very serious view of drug offences. The death penalty is sometimes imposed on drug smugglers, including foreigners, and sometimes on minor traffickers who were found guilty on a second or third offence. Possession of the smallest quantity of drugs can lead to several years in prison, as Bettie found out.

Being jailed in Saudi Arabia is a devastating and uncomfortable experience; its purpose is punishment, not rehabilitation. Prisons are overcrowded and for much of the year are uncomfortably hot. Exercise is often only an occasional privilege. Visitors are allowed although conditions aren't like in the United Kingdom.

Garth and his two children remained in Saudi Arabia. He continued to work at Al-Qahtani at his job in the laboratory. He visited his wife from time to time, but due to the location of the prison his visits were infrequent.

I wasn't surprised at the news about Bettie. Lots of good people get into trouble in Saudi Arabia; it is not difficult to do. I had been introduced to Bettie at a party but didn't know her well.

It was about six months later that I first heard the news about Garth. I was visiting the new pipe coating facility on the north side of Dammam to investigate a coating problem for one of the pipeline groups.

Apparently, Garth had gotten involved with delivering alcohol that had been smuggled into Saudi

Arabia. He was caught with his company pick-up truck full of boxes of alcohol in the suburbs of Dammam.

To the best of my knowledge, Garth wasn't an alcoholic or even a heavy drinker. It seemed to me that there was only one reason Garth would have been involved in such a venture, and that was to make more money. Greed seems to take control of many people. In Britain, for this type of offence, you would probably receive a fine or slap on the wrist. In Saudi Arabia, it is a serious offence which would result in a jail term and possibly a heavy fine as well. The Saudi justice system tries to make an example out of these people, as a deterrent to others.

Very little information was ever received about Garth, except that he received a four-year jail term. Now that both he and his wife were in prison, their children were shipped back to relatives in the United Kingdom. A sad ending to an overseas career and experience which could have set the family up for financial stability when they eventually returned home. Now, they'll only have bad memories and financial hardships as a result of their time in the kingdom of Saudi Arabia.

First home at Sea View, Al-Khobar.

Second home, North Camp, or Moon Base Charley.

Dhahran Hospital Washroom Poster.

Placard at Lucky Well No. 7.

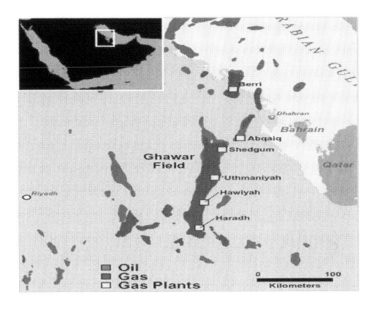

Ghahwr Field

Ras Tanura Refinery

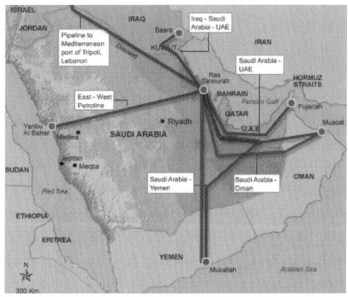

East West Pipeline. Shedgum to Yanbu

Landing at the Heli pad near Golf Course Boulevard in Dhahran, for the trip to the Aramco repair barge ARB-1.

Coming into land on the Aramco repair barge
ARB-1.

The Kings Palace north of Dhahran.

Concrete coated pipe sections for an undersea
pipeline being welded together on the lay barge.

Concrete coated pipe being lowered into the ocean
off the lay barge.

Clown Fish

Lion Fish

The Camel Market in Hofuf.

The Camel Market in Hofuf.

The potter at work in his cave near Hofuf.

The Judas cave

Dive trip to Juraid Island by dhow.

Hot Hot Hot. No air conditioning on this vessel on the way back from Juraid Island.

CHAPTER 18

A Visitor From England

My first wife lives in the South-West part of England with my daughter Jane, in the same town where I spent my early working years before immigrating to Canada.

I found out that children by a first marriage were entitled to come to the kingdom on a one-time trip to visit the parent. If they were a student attending college or university, Aramco would pay the cost of the airfare. This was too good an opportunity for me to pass up. My daughter would most likely never have the opportunity to visit Saudi Arabia, to see this part of the world and experience the culture of the Middle East. Tourists were not permitted to enter the country at the time.

Jane was attending a college in England so would have two months off from her studies during the summer months. Because she was eighteen at the time, she didn't need her mother's permission. Naturally, her mother was a little apprehensive at first, being concerned for her safety, but decided that her daughter should go, as she would never have this opportunity again. Jane, also, was a bit nervous about travelling on her own and visiting a country so far away.

Jane was enthusiastic about the trip, after making the decision to come. She asked me a number of questions and decided to come for three weeks.

I was delighted, and notified Aramco so that arrangements for her entry and exit permit could commence. Jane's passport was sent to the Saudi Embassy in London. Six weeks later she received the appropriate permit stamps to allow her to enter the kingdom.

I had reminded her about bringing clothing that would cover her arms and legs for trips we would make off camp, and preferably a one-piece swimsuit. It was understandable that Jane wouldn't be able to imagine the type of restrictions placed on women in this Muslim country. It would be an education for her to see first-hand the restricted life for women in the kingdom.

I advised her, that if she had clothing from Marks & Spencer, to cut out the labels because Marks & Spencer is Jewish owned. Saudi Arabia doesn't recognize Israel, and as a result will confiscate Jewish products if found by customs during entry. Maps purchased in Saudi Arabia have Israel blacked out with a felt marker.

Aramco is very generous when it comes to benefits for company employees. When vacationing in many parts of the world, an employee is entitled to ship furniture and souvenirs, that have been purchased, back to Saudi Arabia. Aramco will pay the full cost of packing and shipment. The employee notifies the designated shipping agent in the country of purchase, and the agent will pack and ship the goods to Saudi Arabia. Monica and I took advantage of this several times during our holiday trips to Hong Kong and the Philippines.

Monica and I started making plans for Jane's holiday. We wanted to show her as much as possible during her visit.

"We need to make a list of places to visit," Monica said, "so that on your time off on the weekends we cover the places off camp where I wouldn't be able to take her on my own."

Monica couldn't drive off camp. She had to rely on the Aramco buses to go into the local towns during her time off on weekdays.

Monica opened a notebook she kept and started writing down a few places that she thought we could take Jane: the Aramco beach, Al-Khobar, the swimming pools, the camel market in Al-Hofuf, Juraid Island.

"I know we won't be able to do all these things," she said. "We should try to do as much as possible during her visit because she'll probably never get the chance again."

The only time Jane could come was during the holy month of Ramadan. Ramadan is a time of prayer and fasting that commemorates the divine revelation received by the Prophet Mohammed.

Ramadan is the ninth month of the Muslim Hijri calendar during which the faithful abstain from eating, drinking, smoking and having sex from dawn until sunset. In the evening when the fast is broken, they eat small meals and visit friends and family. It is a time to reflect and worship God. Muslims are expected to put more effort into following the teachings of Islam during Ramadan, and to avoid obscene and irreligious sights and sounds. It is a time for worship and contemplation, and a time to strengthen family and community ties.

The fast is intended to be an exacting act of deep personal worship in which Muslims seek a raised awareness of closeness to God.

Observing Ramadan is one of the five pillars of Islam. The others being the shahada or profession of faith, the obligation to pray five times a day, the giving of alms or zakat and going on pilgrimage to Mecca (the hajj).

The month of Ramadan changes every year. The onset of Ramadan is determined by observing the crescent moon or by astronomical calculations, and can vary from country to country.

The Hijri, or lunar calendar, has eleven fewer days than the Gregorian calendar. As compared to the Gregorian, or solar calendar, the dates of Ramadan vary, moving backward a few days each year.

The first day of the holy month is decided by the sighting of the crescent moon by the naked eye. Theologians and scholars gather every year to determine the onset of Ramadan.

Women who're pregnant or breast-feeding, the sick and travellers all have the right not to observe the fast, but they must do so as soon as they're able.

It is traditional to break the fast with a meal known as iftar, consisting of dates and goat's milk, as the Prophet is said to have done. The last meal before dawn is known as suhur.

The holy month ends with feasting and gifts on Islam's biggest festival, Eid al-Fitr.

The Eid holiday is similar to Christmas.

Pilgrims flock to Islam's holiest sites at Mecca and Medina in Saudi Arabia during the Hajj, particularly on the eighth to twelfth days of Dhu al-Hijjah, the last month of the Islamic calendar. The holiest night is on day 27, marking the revelation of the Koran to the Prophet in 610 AD.

I didn't know if Jane smoked so I made her aware of the restrictions pertaining to Ramadan. I advised her not to smoke eat or drink if her flight arrived at the airport during daylight hours. There are many Muslims from various countries working for Aramco. Non-Muslims are advised by Aramco to respect the Muslim faith by not smoking, eating or drinking in front of Muslims.

During the month of Ramadan, there was always a room in each Aramco department where westerners could go for a smoke, for lunch and for coffee breaks. Here they would be out of sight if they share an office with a Muslim or if their office had windows. Neither Monica nor I were smokers so weren't affected by the smoking restriction.

Jane bought a magazine, at London's Heathrow Airport just before boarding, to read on the long flight over. She picked one that had real-life stories that she enjoyed. It would provide lots of interesting reading to keep her mind occupied between the movies for the eight to nine-hour flight. However, because it was the July issue—a month for the beach and sun tanning—it displayed a photograph of a gorgeous girl in a bikini on the front cover. Naturally she didn't think anything of this at the time. During the long flight, she read her magazine and watched the in-flight movies, and slept a little between brief chats with a lady across the aisle. The passenger on her right seemed to have no trouble sleeping, and except for mealtimes he seemed fast away in dreamland.

Upon arrival at Dhahran Airport, Jane retrieved her carry-on from the overhead compartment and rolled up her magazine and placed it in the side pocket.

I had given her lots of information about what to expect when going through customs and security at Dhahran Airport upon arrival.

"Don't be alarmed if they turn out your bags. They do that to most people; it is not out of the ordinary. Try to keep calm and be courteous," I had advised.

Her suitcase was searched and only a few articles of clothing were pulled out. She was able to repack without any trouble. Next was her carry-on bag. The customs officer looked nothing like a customs officer as he didn't have a uniform. He unzipped the side pocket of her carry-on and pulled out her rolled-up magazine. He preceded to un-roll the magazine and immediately noticed the girl in the bikini on the front cover.

"What's this?" he said in a very stern voice!

Jane stood there feeling very small and very young, expecting that at any minute she would be thrown into a Saudi jail, and fed bread and water for the rest of her life! She said nothing as he frowned and flicked through the pages of the magazine.

"I held my breath," she later told me, "as I didn't know what was coming next."

"Hmmm," was all he said and stuffed the magazine back into the pocket of the carry-on bag, marked both cases with a chalk mark and sent her on her way!

"I was so relieved. All sorts of things were going through my mind. I was so glad to get out of that madhouse, Dad."

"That will be an experience you'll never forget," I said.

"You're right about that."

It reminded me of the time when we returned from our holiday in Greece. I had almost been caught bringing back yeast, a hydrometer and an air trap for making wine.

Early in the morning after Jane's arrival, I took her to the Aramco passport office to have her Identification card made. Without an ID card she wouldn't be able to get back into the Aramco camp if she were to leave. The office was quiet at seven in the morning when we approached the counter; no one was waiting, which was unusual.

"My daughter needs an ID card," I advised the attendant, and handed him the paperwork.

"You come this way please," he advised Jane, and she followed him to the photography office where her photograph was taken.

Aramco identification photographs aren't normally renowned for being good photographs. You're not allowed to smile. It seemed to me that the photographer's only interest is getting a reasonable likeness of the person and completing the task as quickly as possible. My identification photo made me look like I was a fugitive from San Quinten; the only thing missing being the prisoner's number at the bottom.

When Jane and Monica picked up the ID card the next day, she thought her picture was a dreadful shot of her.

"I look so tired and bleary eyed," she said. "I know I was tired from the long trip, and it was early in the morning, but I look like I'm totally exhausted."

On the first weekend we took Jane to Ras Tanura.

"We can visit our friends Shirley and Bill," Monica said, "and spend some time on the beach."

Our friend's home was just a few steps from the ocean, as were all the family homes in Ras Tanura. It was a sought-after place to live, but because of the limited amount of work at the refinery, the Ras Tanura compound was much smaller than that of Dhahran.

I would most probably never get a transfer there because my work wasn't related to refinery maintenance or operations.

Just after we passed through the Dhahran security gate on Thursday morning on our way to Ras Tanura, I pointed out the rusted car that had been placed on top of a jabal. In Arabic, "jabal" means mountain or hill. This particular rock-faced jabal was about a hundred feet in elevation, with steep sides, and for some reason a car was perched on the top of it. No one seemed to know how the car got there. It was one of those strange things that you see, and then take for granted but often wonder about.

The drive to Ras Tanura was an education for Jane.

"I can't believe how some of these people drive," she remarked. "Do you think we're going to make it without getting hit?"

"This is normal," I replied. "I've driven this highway a number of times and it never gets any easier or better. They have a divided highway planned but I'm sure that will be a few years away."

The searing heat of the day made the blacktop shimmer like a mirage of flowing water, as the highway rose and fell through its desert path. The beige dunes seemed washed out by the morning sun which looked like a ball of orange fire in the sky. The sun's perimeter, in the washed-out blue sky, was undefined as a result of the sand in the higher atmosphere.

A herd of shaggy black goats stood by the highway near a small village, as if trying to cross but couldn't make up their minds. As we approached the edge of the village, a dirty white donkey with an orange dye mark on its rump (possibly an identification like a brand) stood in the road as if challenging us to a confrontation. As I slowed the car, he slowly trotted across the road and into the desert.

The village seemed deserted with only the occasional dog or chicken wandering the littered streets, picking up morsels of discarded food from the potholed surface. Many of the buildings were dilapidated, and never seemed to change much from one time to the next whenever I had driven through.

I told Jane the story about the engineer from Ras Tanura who picked up a new employee from the airport in Dhahran. When they stopped off at this small village on the drive back to Ras Tanura, he told him it was Ras Tanura. Apparently he was so horror stricken at the thought of living there, he said "Take me back to the airport." Jane laughed.

"I can see why!"

"When the new highway is built, this village will probably remain a place that time has forgotten. It may eventually be consumed by the desert sand, as the residents move away because there won't be any vehicle traffic from the highway," I suggested.

Just after leaving the village, Jane noticed three camels making their way between the sand dunes.

"Are they wild camels?" she asked.

"No, they're owned by someone," I replied. "All the camels you'll see roaming the desert are mostly owned by the Bedouin. You don't see the Bedouin tents very often now because many tribes have settled in urban areas. The Bedouin lifestyle is very demanding, and as a result many Bedouin have jobs and live in the towns and cities. The camels that you do see are the dromedary with one hump."

"Yes, that's what those were," Jane replied.

"The dromedary is an interesting animal. They live off the desert plants and grass, and the hump is filled with body fat and not water as some people believe. When they can't find food, the body automatically takes fat from the hump to feed the system and keeps the camel going. It is like an emergency food supply."

"Camels have been known to drink twenty-five gallons of water in ten minutes. Their thirsty blood vessels absorb and carry the water to every part of the body very quickly after they've finished drinking."

"That's really interesting, Dad. I always thought the hump was full of water."

We stopped to take pictures and video footage several times on the way to Ras Tanura so didn't arrive until almost midday.

When we arrived at the Najmah residential compound, the security guard at the gate checked our identification and waved us through.

It was a short drive through the paved tree-lined streets of the compound to our friend's home. In Arabic, Ras Tanura means "Cape Oven", possibly due to the high temperatures of the cape that projects out into the sea.

As we opened the car doors to greet our friends, Shirley and Bill, we felt a cool breeze blowing in from the ocean. It was a welcome relief from the high midday temperature of one hundred and eight degrees.

"It's a hot one," Bill said. "Come on in. We have lunch ready and the house is a lot cooler than outside."

After lunch, we spent the afternoon on the beach, body surfing in the waves and relaxing under the shade of a large umbrella. The water temperature was eighty-five degrees.

"It feels like lukewarm bath water," Jane remarked.

It was too hot to sit in the sun for long without getting burnt to a crisp. Frequent dips in the ocean and the cool ocean breeze kept us relatively comfortable until late afternoon. Bill lit the barbecue to cook an early supper of Hamour which he had purchased from the local fish market. Aramco provided barbecues at a number of locations along the beach. You just have to bring your own briquettes and lighter fluid.

Hamour is a brown-spotted grouper found in the Arabian Gulf area, and is a fish often favoured by Aramcons. Shirley had prepared it with onion, tomato, garlic, hot peppers and cumin, laid on a bed of rice and garnished with limes. It was all wrapped in several layers of tinfoil so all that Bill had to do was turn it over a few times until it was cooked.

It was starting to cool off a little. A few families arrived and were enjoying the beach with their children, and some were also organizing and preparing the evening meal.

"It is a beautiful beach and never crowded like the beaches back home," Shirley remarked. "We feel very fortunate and lucky to be living here. I hope Bill doesn't get transferred to another refinery because we would really miss this beach and lifestyle."

After a leisurely supper, we roasted marshmallows over the hot coals on the barbecue. Shirley carved up a huge watermelon into slices for dessert to accompany the fresh dates that were so delicious and plentiful at their local market.

The drive back to Dhahran was uneventful, the end of a memorable day. The desert was starting to take on a new look as the sun began to sink in the western sky. The washed-out beige of the dunes as seen on our trip up was being replaced by many shades of brown and gold. The dunes were taking on more defined shapes as shadows started to creep across the sand. Ripples and undulations not previously seen in the morning sun were becoming apparent. The occasional camel tracks could be seen meandering through the sand, and the desert shrubs were casting long shadows against the golden backdrop.

As the sun sank below the horizon, twilight lasted for about thirty minutes before it faded into darkness. The desert once again took on a fresh new look of shadowy forms. Another day in the desert was coming to an end.

Most afternoons whilst I was at work, Monica and Jane would take Blaine to the pool. He was two years old, but could swim quite well thanks to a swimming program that Aramco organized. Two swimming instructors were brought in from the United States to put on a number of instructional programs for various age groups and level of ability. Blaine was able to take the beginners class for children which was comprised of six lessons. The lessons, held in the evening when it was cooler, enabled me to assist. Blaine wasn't afraid of water, and had lots of fun with the six other children in the program. He was able to follow all the instructions and didn't mind when he sank below the surface. At one part of the program, the children were dropped off the diving board into the water at the deep end to get them accustomed to being underwater. I caught Blaine when he bobbed up to the surface. He thought that was tremendous fun and wasn't afraid at all. By age five Blaine was swimming the width of the pool, although he seemed to like swimming underwater for most of the width.

I also took a series of lessons in the adult class to improve my stroke and technique.

"I can't believe how well he swims," Jane said. "He's like a little fish; he is amazing for his age."

Blaine loved the water and always looked forward to his trip to the pool. Although he could swim quite well, Monica wouldn't let him go in the water on his own. He couldn't touch the bottom in the shallow end. He splashed around with Jane and threw his ball around with her, and never seemed to want to get out when it was time to go home. Even though there was a sunshade over the pool and the water ran through a chiller, the water felt a comfortable lukewarm.

Monica and I made lots of new friends, some as a result of our work and others from Monica's association with other children at Blaine's daycare. We also made friends through evening programs that Aramco would organize. New people were arriving all the time because of attrition, and most people were eager to make new friends because they'd left all their friends and relatives behind.

I met Frazer when I was working in the Dhahran purchasing department. He was a tall man of about six foot three, a little overweight, quiet spoken and wore rimless spectacles. He was recruited out of Foster Wheeler, an international construction company, from their office in Minneapolis, and arrived in Saudi Arabia about four months ahead of me. Frazer's wife, Kim, was from Japan. She'd met Frazer when he was serving in the United States Forces. Kim was a typical Japanese lady—short, slim, with black shoulder-length hair and dark complexion. They had two children, Cinda and Josh, who resembled their mother in many ways, and were very well behaved and polite. I wondered if this was typical of the Japanese heritage or had they just been taught well by their parents!

Kim was an excellent cook, and often made traditional Japanese meals for the family to be eaten with chopsticks.

Monica and I enjoyed their company and socialized with them on a number of occasions. Sometimes, Monica and Kim and the children would meet at the pool. This gave the children the opportunity to enjoy each other's company as they were all about the same age. When Kim found out that my daughter was coming for a visit, she invited us over to their home for dinner. Frazer and Kim were still in temporary housing on camp and lived within walking distance of us.

"You must bring Jane over for dinner," Kim said. "I'll cook a traditional Japanese meal for her if she would like that."

"I'm sure she would," Monica replied. "We will look forward to that."

The following day at lunch time, I phoned Monica to see if she would like to go to the beach after I finished work.

"We're going to the beach tonight when Mark gets home from work," she told Jane, "so put on your swimming costume. We'll have our supper on the beach, barbecue chicken, is that OK?"

"Sounds wonderful Monica. Can I help you prepare anything?"

"I'll make us a salad, so you can help chop the tomatoes and cucumber if you like."

Blaine decided he wanted to help, so Jane gave him a piece of cucumber to play with whilst she washed and sliced the vegetables for the salad.

"How long does it take to get to the beach?" Jane asked.

"About twenty minutes, it's not far. We'll load up the car so that we can go as soon as Mark returns from work."

When I arrived in my truck, they were ready to set off. I quickly changed into a T-shirt and shorts.

I had purchased a Plymouth Fury from a Saudi contractor who purchased the old Aramco cars and resold them. The cars and trucks were in reasonable condition, and I knew they'd been serviced regularly as was Aramco's policy. They were not high mileage vehicles. The cars were generally white so that they reflected the sun, and had the basic necessities like air-conditioning, cruise control and a radio. Aramco kept the cars for about a year and a half to two years, and then sold them off when their new shipment arrived. Most of the vehicles were pool cars. If you needed a car for a few hours you checked one out by giving your department identification and employee number. My car had vinyl seats that get extremely hot when the vehicle is parked in the sun. I threw a rug over both the front and back seats to protect bare legs from getting burnt.

We arrived at the beach at about five-thirty. The road along the beachfront is about a mile long with vehicle parking behind the beach sunshades that Aramco had provided.

There were about twenty sunshades along the beach, and under each was a picnic table and a barbecue. During weekdays there was generally a sunshade available. On weekends, it sometimes got crowded but you could generally find a table and sunshade to share with another family. At the end of the beach road were large sand dunes that came down to the ocean. Beyond the sand dunes about half a mile away, the Aramco yacht club provided moorage for boat lovers and sailors. A number of small boats and yachts were moored at the marina, bobbing in the gentle breeze.

I found a vacant sunshade and parked the car. We unloaded our picnic hamper and barbecue briquettes. Jane strapped on Blaine's water wings and they were soon in the water splashing around and having lots of fun.

I lit the barbecue and went in for a quick swim whilst the coals got hot. I had become accustomed to the salinity in the Gulf of Arabia which resulted in very good buoyancy. It seemed almost impossible to sink. I would lie on my back and relax bobbing in the gentle swell of the lukewarm water.

Monica had put the potatoes on the barbecue to bake just before I came out of the water, and was preparing the chicken with spices and barbecue sauce. The carrots, onions and broccoli, which were wrapped in tinfoil, had to be placed on the grill when I started cooking the chicken.

The sun was starting to sink in the west and had lost some of its heat when we sat down to supper. However, it was still about ninety-five degrees under the sunshade roof. We were all wet from our swim, and the light breeze gave a cooling effect as we enjoyed our meal with a fruit punch that Monica had prepared that afternoon.

"The only thing missing here," Jane said, "is a nice glass of wine."

"You've got that right," I replied, "A cold beer would not go amiss either."

This would be the first of several trips to the Aramco beach that Jane would enjoy during her stay in Saudi Arabia. Having a barbecue on the beach was a new experience for her. Although she'd grown up living only a short distance from the ocean, it was something that's not normally done in the United Kingdom. Perhaps due to the cooler weather, crowded beaches and lack of facilities.

Jane only had three weeks in Saudi Arabia so Monica and I wanted to pack as much into her stay as possible. It is not a country that caters to tourists but there are many things to see and do that we wanted her to experience.

One evening I drove her to Al-Khobar to visit the gold souks.

The shopping area of Al-Khobar is often quite busy in the evenings with many nationalities shopping for a variety of goods and services. Most of the streets are laid out in blocks similar to North America. The streets tend to be narrow, and open to traffic. This adds to the general congestion of people walking in all directions, both on narrow sidewalks and on the streets. Many of the streets and sidewalks are in a state of disrepair. Broken blacktop, possibly due in part to the extreme heat, and broken concrete sidewalks are common. Many of the streets contain deep potholes. Most of the buildings in the shopping area are single or two storey. Many of the retail shops have steel mesh-type security blinds that can be quickly drawn down at closing time, or for prayer break at around seven in the evening.

Sidewalk food is common, but of questionable hygiene. Street vendors carve lamb from a vertical roasting spit into a pita pocket called a shawarma, a local delicacy. Flies sometimes pitch on the lamb as it rotates and roasts. It is anyone's guess if the vendor's hands are clean as he handles the pita bread and waves his arms to keep away the flies.

Ford cars aren't imported into Saudi Arabia, partly due to the Arab boycotts of companies dealing with Israel. Many years ago, Fords must have been allowed into the country because I came across an Aramco engineer in Dhahran Hills who was restoring a 1955 Thunderbird.

One evening, when a friend, Pat Miller, and I were shopping for Christmas presents for our children in Al-Khobar, Pat ushered me into the back of a toy store and said: "Take a look at this."

Pat put his hand behind a box containing a toy car, and pulled out a car sitting unboxed at the back of the shelf and showed it to me. It was a zinc die-cast model of an American car, and had the word Ford written on it.

"I bet that has been there for a long time," he said. "I wonder what would happen if we were to try and buy it?"

He put the car back behind the box where he found it.

There are a number of gold souks in Al-khobar and their pricing didn't vary much. Gold is sold by the ounce, according to the fluctuating price of gold on the stock market.

"All of the gold in the souks is eighteen carat or better," I explained to my daughter. "We'll buy you a bracelet or necklace to take home. The prices here are much better than anything you would find in the United Kingdom. We'll go to several souks. Keep an eye out for something you like, and then we'll go back and buy it after we've done our tour. You'll find that a lot of the gold jewellery is very gaudy, and not something the average westerner would wear."

Jane was awestruck at the first window we looked in; she'd never seen so much gold hanging from display stands and in window cases. We entered the store and browsed through the glass-topped cases. The store was quite busy with a number of Saudi ladies in black veils chattering in Arabic, and trying on bracelets and bangles. There were also a number of westerners and other nationalities shopping for gold.

"It's a busy place," Jane remarked. "I can't believe all this gold. Some of those Saudi women seem to be wearing a lot of perfume," she whispered.

Jane found a necklace with a pendant that she liked. We wanted to look around in other gold shops before making a decision so we didn't try to barter on the price of three hundred and forty-five riyals.

When we left the shop, I said, "We can probably get that necklace for around two hundred and ninety riyals. They expect you to barter. So if that's the one you decide on, we'll go back and negotiate the price."

We went to two other gold shops that were equally as crowded with shoppers. There was a good selection of necklaces which Jane had decided she would like rather than a bracelet. The sales people spoke good English in all of the gold shops we visited. In the last shop, the salesperson was determined to make a sale. He held up a mirror for Jane to see the necklace she tried on.

"Special price for you," he said. "You like? I can also make you a necklace that has your name written in Arabic."

He reached under the counter and produced a necklace that he had made for another customer as an example. "It would take one week to make," he said.

"I really like that, Dad. How much would it cost?"

He asked Jane to write her name down on a note pad he had on the counter, and then he wrote her name in Arabic beside it.

"I can have it made for four hundred and sixty-five riyals," he said.

Monica was looking at the bracelets whilst Jane and I were trying to decide on a necklace. She'd found a beautiful three-strand bracelet with very delicately platted strands of red, yellow and white gold. She passed it to Jane to try on.

"How much for the bracelet?" I asked.

He took the bracelet and weighed it and said, "One hundred and eighty."

I did a quick calculation in my head and realized that for both the necklace and bracelet it was about two hundred and twenty-five dollars Canadian. I thought I could get about ten to fifteen percent off that price, and offered him five hundred and fifty. He shook his head and thought about it for a few seconds and said, "Six hundred."

"Five eighty," I countered.

"You drive a hard bargain, siddiq! For the lady, OK."

He put the bracelet in a box and made out a receipt.

"You pay for the bracelet and fifty percent deposit for the necklace, OK?"

"Yes, that will be OK," I replied.

"Come back in one week and I'll have the necklace for you." I shook his hand, and we left.

"You never know if you're getting a good deal or not," I said as we left the shop. "Dealing is a tradition with them; they're very good at it. They expect it on all goods, and they enjoy doing it like a sport."

"Thanks, Dad," Jane said. "I'll cherish that, and will remember you and him bargaining every time I wear it."

It was dark when we drove back to Dhahran and Blaine fell asleep as soon as he felt the jiggling motion of the vehicle. The array of neon, haphazard street lighting, honking of horns, people jaywalking all over the streets, and the various smells that waft in the hot night air are typical in this little town. It is a hive of activity in the evening. We quickly left the downtown area behind, and were soon making our way through the dimly lit residential suburbs of Al-Khobar and back on to the highway to Dhahran.

* * * * *

It was mid-June when the Dhahran Dive Club decided to take another trip to Juraid Island. I had been there before. Although it was a long day, I enjoyed my previous trip with the abundance of tropical fish in the coral reef around the tiny island.

When I told Jane about the trip, she was eager to go. It would be the only opportunity she would have to see the region's tropical fish, and also go on an Arabian dhow.

I had filled up my diving tank with compressed air at the Aramco Dive Club compressor station on the Wednesday evening, in preparation for an early departure the following morning.

"We have to be up really early," I advised Jane. "The Aramco Greyhound bus, that will take us to the port of Jubail, leaves the commissary parking lot at six-thirty sharp."

"There is a toilet on the bus," I advised Jane. "And I think there is one at the port. But after we board the dhow, there won't be a toilet, so be aware of that. Once we get to the island and you're in the water you can pee in the ocean. Not the best, but beggars can't be choosers."

"I'll keep that in mind," Jane replied. "Will Blaine be coming with us?" she asked.

"No, we'll take him to our friends, Garth and Danielle Fenton. They said they would have him for the day. They have two young boys, Garth Junior and James, so he'll have someone to play with. It would be too long a trip for him, and besides the lack of toilet facilities would be a problem."

We'd packed everything the night before, and were up at five on the Thursday morning. After Blaine had finished his breakfast, Monica put him in the pushchair with his day's provisions and pushed him the five blocks to the Fenton's home.

The bus was in the parking lot when I parked my car beneath the shade of a large tree. I unloaded my diving equipment and our bags from the trunk. There were a number of people on the bus already when Monica and Jane climbed aboard with their carry-on bags. They found a seat near the middle of the bus.

The bus driver, who was from the Philippines, helped me load my diving bag into the storage compartment under the bus. Many of the Aramco bus drivers were from the Philippines and were generally very helpful and sociable. He said his name was Claudio. We stood chatting for a while until more passengers arrived.

Monica and I took the opportunity to get some extra sleep on the trip up to Jubail. Jane found the trip interesting as it was all new for her. She passed the time reading several articles about the history and people of Arabia in a magazine that Monica had found for her.

When the bus arrived at the Port of Jubail, it stopped at the security gate for a guard to come on board and do a head count. The security barrier was lifted and the bus proceeded to the dock where several fishing dhows were tied up at the wharf.

"Last chance for the washroom," I whispered in Jane's ear.

"Right Dad," and she headed to the lineup at the back of the bus.

It was shaping up to be another hot day. There was a light breeze from the south as the dhow chugged its way out of the mouth of Jubail harbour. Seagulls followed the dhow as it made its way out to sea. They came so close to the dhow that they could be fed bits of bread from the outstretched hands of passengers.

They'd obviously done this before, I thought. *They know where the food is.*

All the passengers were seated on the deck of the dhow with their backs resting against the gunwale—not the most comfortable way to travel. The dhow was built for fishing, not for transporting passengers, and as a result had very few creature comforts on board. It was the month of Ramadan when Muslims fast during the hours of daylight. Jane noticed that one of the Saudi fishermen at the wheel was smoking, and whispered to me: "I thought they weren't supposed to smoke during Ramadan!"

"They can if they're travelling," I replied. "So if you want to eat or drink, it is acceptable to do so. They'll break the fast during our trip, for as long as we're out to sea."

"Oh, I didn't know that," Jane replied. "I'm dying for a drink."

"Help yourself. There is lots of cold ice water in the cooler in the green bag beside Monica. Cups are in the side pocket."

We were soon out of sight of land. The seagulls had given up on their food supply and must have headed back to land.

"Hey, what the heck is that climbing up that locker?" Jane pointed to a rectangular box on the deck next to the mast.

"They're cockroaches. You'll see lots of them on these dhows; they're infested with them. They've been on all the dhows that I've been on."

"They're generally nocturnal, but I've noticed that they're always crawling around during the daytime on the dhows. However, I believe that there are different types, and some are attracted to light, so perhaps they're a different species to those in North America."

Because it's just a sandbar with very little elevation, Juraid Island seemed to come up suddenly from out of nowhere. There is virtually no vegetation except for scattered clumps of wild grass. The captain anchored the dhow with its bow into the slight current and next to the coral reef. He threw a rope ladder with wooden treads over both sides of the vessel to facilitate entry and exit by the swimmers. He proceeded to lie down in a shady area with a cushion for his head to have a nap.

In no time at all everyone was in the water. The swimmers and snorkelers got off the dhow on the port side on the inside of the coral reef where the water was shallower. The dive club members entered the water on the starboard side on the outside of the reef. The coral wall dropped off to a depth of about thirty-five feet. The coral reef was only about seventy-five feet from the shore of the tiny island, and the water shallow enough to stand when ten feet inside the reef.

Jane and Monica had taken some bread buns in a net bag into the water to feed the fish. They were soon surrounded by brightly coloured angelfish, several varieties of butterfly fish, black spotted grunts, and many other colourful species. They had to stop feeding them because they became completely surrounded by fish. They could see nothing but fish in all directions, and could feel them gently nibbling at their skin with their tiny mouths. Jane had never seen seahorses before, and found them fascinating to watch as they floated by in a vertical position with their tails curled up.

They looked so dainty and surreal, she thought.

Jim, my friend from Vancouver, and I were enjoying our dive on the coral reef wall. The bottom was sand and uninteresting, so we explored the jagged coral wall, looking at all its inhabitants. A variety of large and small fish were in abundance around the reef. They were inquisitive and playful with us. The smaller fish seemed to delight in playing with the exhausted air bubbles as they floated from our air regulators to the surface. I had a small problem with my air regulator free flowing, and thought it could be attributed to the current exerting pressure on the purge button of my regulator. I was able to eliminate the problem when I switched my Scuba-Pro regulator to "pre-dive". I noticed that I had to breathe in a little harder in the "pre-dive" position, which is normal, but at least I wasn't wasting air.

After our dive, Jim and I relaxed in the shade for a while and filled out our diving logbooks. My book noted:

Water temperature: 86 degrees Fahrenheit.
Visibility: 30 feet.
Maximum depth of dive: 35 feet.
Bottom time: 1 hour.
Air temperature: 108 degrees Fahrenheit.
Time out of water: 12:00 noon.
Decompression: nil.
Total underwater hours accumulated to date: 8.25 hours.
Diving buddy: Jim McColl.

When one of the other divers surfaced on the port side of the dhow, he shouted to the swimmers on the inside of the reef that there were sharks on the other side of the dhow.

Jane said after her swim that when she heard the diver's announcement, she felt weirdly calm but decided to get out of the water.

"I watched the movie Jaws a few years ago and it scared the crap out of me," she remarked.

Monica also got out of the water, as did nearly all of the swimmers.

"Perhaps we didn't feel that there was safety in numbers," she remarked.

"They were probably nurse sharks which often dwell near the sea floor," I advised. "Could also have been grey reef sharks. They are generally sighted in the shallower waters near the drop-off of a coral reef. Although, last year we were visited by a tiger shark during a deep dive near this island. I didn't see it, but the other divers I was with said it circled around Jim and me and then left. Probably thought we would be too tough a meal!"

After lunch, Monica, Jane, Jim and I swam ashore to explore the island.

"Sea turtles nest here," Jim said, "but you probably won't see any. I believe they're Hawksbill or Green turtles. They come ashore, dig a hole and deposit about 80 to 150 eggs, and then they fill the nest back in with sand and crawl back into the sea. The eggs incubate and hatch in the hot sand. The temperature of the sand plays a role in the sex of the hatchlings."

"You seem very knowledgeable about turtles," Jane remarked.

"Not really. I read an article recently about them in a National Geographic magazine I got from the library."

We took a thirty-minute tour of the island which consisted of scattered wild grass and low sand dunes.

Very uninteresting but worth the walk, Jane thought.

At two-thirty the captain asked everyone to return to the dhow and started to make preparations to leave.

"Don't dry yourself with a towel. Keep wet for as long as possible," I advised Jane, "so that you'll remain cool for as long as possible. It is going to be a hot trip back."

Everyone found a place to sit on the deck again as the captain pulled the anchor and hauled in the rope ladders.

"That was fun." Jane said. "I really enjoyed that; I'm glad we were able to come. It's a trip I will always remember."

"I think it's time for a snack. Anyone else want a granola bar?" Monica asked.

Everyone seemed to have the same idea—relaxing on the deck with drinks and refreshments.

The dhow headed back to Jubail in the scorching heat of the afternoon sun. Jane read a magazine that she'd brought along for the trip. She found herself nodding off to sleep after a while aided by the gentle rocking of the dhow and the rhythmic vibrations from its engine.

It was close to five o'clock when we chugged our way into Jubail harbour and tied up at the wharf. Claudio was waiting beside our bus. He helped unload our diving equipment and stored it in the baggage compartment of the bus. He had started the bus just before we docked so the air conditioner had had a chance to cool the interior before we boarded. Everyone appreciated that. The bus had been sitting in the sun all day and had probably been like an oven inside.

The security guard stopped the bus at the harbour gate. He came aboard to do a head count as part of his security check before signalling the driver with a wave of his hand to proceed past the raised barrier. I sat next to my friend Jim and chatted about our dive and Jim's upcoming repat. Jim was divorced from his wife but had met an old school friend at a class reunion during his last trip home. He had married her before his return. He had made arrangements to bring her to Arabia but it had taken longer than expected to get her an entry permit. He was looking forward to bringing her back to Arabia. He had just moved into his permanent home in Dhahran Hills.

I noticed that Monica was fast asleep with a novel in her lap, and Jane looked like she was ready to nod off as she read her magazine.

"I see from my diving log book that we've made three trips to Juraid Island," Jim said. "A lot of the dive club members are going over to Yanbu on the Red Sea; we'll have to look into that. I believe we can get one of Aramco's aircraft over and back, and camp on the beach, so it will cost us very little to go."

"That sounds like a fun weekend," I replied. "We'll have to get some more information on that from the dive club."

I rested my head against the seat back and fell asleep.

Jane's holiday in Saudi Arabia was coming to an end. She had four more days left before her flight back to the United Kingdom. I remembered that friends, Frazer and Kim, had invited us over for dinner before Jane returned home, as Kim was going to cook Jane a typical Japanese meal. Monica and Kim met at the commissary the next day and arranged the dinner for the following evening. It would be a farewell dinner for Jane, and also a chance for her to experience a little Japanese hospitality. When I told Jane about the dinner plans she felt sad that she was leaving, but was looking forward to meeting Frazer and Kim and their two children, Cinda and Josh.

"I've never had real Japanese food," she said. "It will be a new experience for me. I'm looking forward to that."

Frazer and Kim were still in their temporary housing in Dhahran, in a house similar to ours and only about six blocks away. Jane had bought a box of chocolates for Kim and gave it to her when all the family greeted us at the door. Kim was dressed in a traditional Japanese kimono, blue with a floral design and a red waistband. Cinda, who was four years old, was also wearing a kimono and had her black hair tied up with two red ribbons.

She looked like a little doll, Jane thought.

We sat around on cushions on the floor with a low coffee table between us and sampled some of Frazer's homemade beer.

"I've been making beer for about a year now," he said, "ever since we moved into Dhahran. It seems to turn out not too bad. What do you think Mark?"

"I like it," I replied. "I've not had a beer since our last repat; you'll have to show me how to make it."

Kim had laid the table with placemats, brightly coloured napkins, Japanese-style soup bowls, spoons and chopsticks. She said we could have knives and forks if we wished.

The traditional way of sitting at a Japanese dining table for both men and women, is in the seiza position with your legs folded beneath you. I found this too uncomfortable and sat cross-legged, as did Frazer. Monica sat with her legs out to one side.

Kim had been in the kitchen preparing dinner. She brought in a large bowl of miso soup with tofu, served it into the soup bowls and sat down.

"Itadakimasu," she said. "That means I gratefully receive. It's Japanese custom to say that before eating."

Blaine was sitting in his pushchair beside the table, and screwed up his face when Monica gave him a taste. Kim had prepared a number of dishes that she brought in from the kitchen when we finished our soup. Goyza dumplings, domburi rice, yakitori chicken on skewers, tonkatsu (deep fried pork cutlets with cabbage) and norimaki (sushi rice and seafood). She explained what everything was, and indicated that she was limited to what dishes she could make as some of the ingredients weren't available in Saudi Arabia.

"It's nice that Aramco has the pork store in the commissary for non-Muslims, as it does give us some variety of meats," I remarked.

"Muslims don't eat pork because the flesh of swine is considered to be unclean, and strongly forbidden in Islam," I explained to Jane. "Eating pork is regarded as an extremely unholy act. Aramco has the pork store where we can get bacon, pork roasts, chops, ribs and sausages but we're limited to a fixed amount each month. When we reach the limit, we have to wait until the next month to buy more. We don't often reach our limit. Some of the British fellows, that I work with in the companies I visit in Dammam, sometimes ask if I can get them some bacon or sausages. It doesn't happen often, so I generally oblige if I have quota left that I'll not use. I'm not supposed to do that, and I'm sure Aramco would take a dim view of it if they found out. British people like their bacon and sausages for breakfast."

"I'm sorry I don't have any sake to offer you," Frazer said. "I may try making it sometime as it is made by a brewing process similar to beer, but brewed from rice. It would be interesting to try it."

Frazer and Kim had many questions for Jane about her holiday in Saudi Arabia, and wished her a safe trip home. Her return flight was only two days away now.

"I'll be sad to leave," she said. "I'm so glad I came, and thank you for this wonderful evening and delicious meal. I really enjoyed everything."

Blaine was happily playing with Cinda and Josh, and all their toys, and didn't want to leave.

"I can see that he is a night owl," Kim said. "Typical little boy."

He was fast asleep in his pushchair by the time we arrived home.

Jane wasn't looking forward to her trip home.

"Going home is never as nice as leaving on holiday," she said. "But it will be nice not to have the restrictions that exist in Saudi Arabia, especially during Ramadan."

Ramadan wasn't yet over, but would be in a few more days.

"Fasting must be difficult for them," she said. "Especially for the people who have to work outside in the hot sun all day."

I had picked up Jane's passport at the Aramco passport office on the Tuesday, and checked to see that she had the exit permit stamp. It covered one complete page. Without that stamp she wouldn't be permitted to leave the kingdom.

On Thursday morning, Jane packed her suitcase in preparation for the trip home that evening. Her flight on British Airways was scheduled to leave Dhahran at 10:55 p.m., and was a direct flight to London Heathrow arriving in the early morning the following day.

After supper, Jane took a shower to freshen up for her trip, and phoned home to advise her mother that she was all packed and ready to leave for the airport. Her mother and stepfather had arranged to pick her up at the airport.

Monica and I gave Jane a big hug and kiss before we left the house.

"I can't hug and kiss at the airport," I advised her. "The Saudis would take a dim view of that, especially as it is Ramadan. If there are any Matawa (religious police) at the airport, I run the risk of being arrested."

It was only a thirty-minute drive to the airport but we'd left in lots of time. Jane had to be at the airport three hours ahead of her flight time.

We entered the terminal building and went to the check-in desk. There was only one other person ahead of Jane so we only had a few minutes to wait. All passengers checked in at the same desk, which is a little different to that of other airports. Her ticket and passport were checked, a boarding pass and checked luggage receipt issued, and she was instructed to go to the boarding area through the door behind her.

We chatted for a little while. Jane gave Blaine a big hug and kiss, and said "Bye Dad." Then she turned and went through the door to the boarding area, and was gone.

CHAPTER 19

Permanent Housing

It was about six months after Jane's departure that the Aramco housing department called and left a message at my office. I was in Dammam at the time, so didn't get the message until the following day when I went into the office for an early morning meeting. After the meeting, I returned the call.

I wonder what they want, I thought, as I was dialling the number.

After I identified myself, I was put through to another lady.

"Mr Carlile?"

"Yes," I replied.

"This is Kristin. I have some good news for you. Aramco has permanent housing ready for you. You can move during the next two weeks."

I was stunned; I wasn't expecting that, it was the furthest thing from my mind.

"Mr Carlile, are you there?"

"Yes, yes," I replied. "That's great news, thank you." Kristin gave me the address of the house, which was in Dhahran Hills, and said I could go to look at it. The keys could be picked up from the housing office on Tuesday after they'd completed the cleaning. She advised me that I would get a day off work on the moving day, and to advise her later when that would be. As soon as I put down the phone, I picked it up again, and phoned the physiotherapy department at the hospital to give Monica the good news. She was treating a patient at the time, but because it was her husband calling, the receptionist advised me to hold for a few moments whilst they called her. Monica was delighted with the news.

"That's made my day," she said.

"We won't have the keys for two more days but we can drive down and see it after I finish work," I replied.

Jim overheard the conversation and congratulated me on the news. Jim and Annette DeAngelo had been offered permanent housing several months earlier, but declined. They preferred to stay in their temporary home in Dhahran rather than moving to Dhahran Hills. They liked being close enough to walk to everything, and didn't have to use a car.

Aramco had built about two hundred and fifty new homes in Dhahran Hills during the past few years, and many more were in the planning and construction phase. Many of the homes were the standard gable-roofed bungalows. Recently, adobe-style homes with the traditional flat roof were being built with stucco exteriors, similar to homes found in New Mexico.

After work, I picked up Monica and Blaine and drove down to Dhahran Hills to see our new home. It was about a fifteen-minute drive from our temporary home.

It took a little longer because we had to drive around the new construction areas in the Hills to find our street. Some of the new roads were still unpaved but sidewalks had been laid in most areas. The paving is probably the last to be completed. When we located Hasyan Way, there were only homes built on one side of the road; the other side was flat, open desert.

Our new home was a side-by-side adobe style two-storey home with a brown rustic stucco finish and a flat roof. We couldn't get in because it was locked, but were able to look in the windows to get some idea of the interior. It had a small gated front yard, and gated rear yard with high privacy walls. Grass had been planted at the back and front, and had been recently watered because the sandy ground appeared damp. There was a small paved patio at the rear with two sets of sliding glass doors opening on to it. Through one set of doors, we could see what looked like the dining room with the kitchen beyond. Through the other set of doors, there was a large lounge with French doors leading to what looked like a family room.

"It looks big," Monica said. "We'll have to buy some new furniture to fill that. Our one settee and chair will look lost in there."

At the front there was a single-car garage with a driveway that sloped to the street. It looked like our neighbour had already moved in because there was a maroon car in the driveway. I noticed that the upper floor windows had louvered sunshades. They appeared to be fixtures that were made of wood and sat at a slight angle to the window.

A large air-conditioning unit was located just inside the front gate, and was running.

Before we left Dhahran Hills, we drove around to find the home that James and Janet O'Leary had just moved into. Janet was a physiotherapist and worked with Monica at the hospital; James was a teacher at the Dhahran Hills Primary School. They were from Boston and had arrived in Dhahran about two months ahead of Monica and me. By coincidence, their home was identical to ours and was on the next street behind our home.

I remembered Monica telling me about a trip James and Janet made to Al-Khobar one day. Janet had had her second child a few months before, and was starting to lose some of the excess weight that she'd gained as a result of her pregnancy. She was excited to be able to squeeze into her blue jeans again, and wore them to Al-Khobar on a shopping trip with James and the two children. Just before entering a toy store, the Matawa (religious police) stopped James and gave him a lecture about the disgusting manner in which his wife was dressed.

"Your wife's clothing is much too tight and revealing," they told him. "If she comes out in public in such disgusting dress again, you'll be arrested and thrown in jail."

James was shocked at this revelation, as he hadn't given Janet's clothes a second thought before leaving home. When they finally got into the toy store, they had a good chuckle about it.

"It's great that they live behind us," Monica said. "We won't have far to go to visit, or perhaps babysit for one another."

When we arrived back at our temporary home, it suddenly seemed small and dingy.

"When are we moving?" Monica asked. "I want to move as soon as possible."

After supper we talked about what we had to do to make the move.

"We have to send all of our rental furniture back to the furniture warehouse," I said. "Perhaps after work tomorrow you can go to the warehouse and arrange that, and select furniture for our new home."

We made a furniture list, and decided to move on the Wednesday. I would have three full days off before starting back to work on the Saturday.

We didn't have a lot to do. The furniture warehouse would do the pickup and delivery of the furniture. We only had to pack our clothing, food, bedding, kitchenware, Blaine's toys and our personal items. I wasn't supposed to use my company truck for personal trips, but for moving house I was able to get permission from my supervisor to use it. It made a big difference to the number of trips we had to make.

The move on Wednesday went according to plan. By mid-afternoon we were moved into our new home, and had returned the key for our temporary home to the housing department.

Our new rental furniture had been delivered and put into the appropriate rooms. We only had to organize where in the rooms the furniture had to be placed. It was a long day, but by mid-evening everything was unpacked and put away. Blaine thought it was great fun, and liked his bedroom with the new experience of wall-to-wall carpeting. He unpacked all of his toys and spread them out on the floor whilst I assembled his plastic play tent in the corner of the room.

We had a telephone in the master bedroom and one in the kitchen, and both were working the day we moved in. Local calls were free, but we were charged for the long distance calls on a monthly basis, similar to North America.

Rather than permanently rent all of our furniture, we chose a sitting room suite from the J.C. Penney catalogue in the library. It consisted of a chesterfield, two chairs with separate foot rests, two end tables, a coffee table, a bar and two bar stools. Aramco shipped it from Houston to Dhahran at no charge, another nice benefit that Aramco provided to North American employees. It took about eight weeks to arrive, and was well packed and had no damage. If shipping damage had occurred, Aramco would repair or replace the damaged item.

Monica and I had met an American at a friend's home. He'd shipped all of his household furniture and belongings to Dhahran when he moved into permanent housing. It was all lost during shipping. The container ship, that their furniture was on, encountered bad weather on the trip to Saudi Arabia. A number of shipping containers moved on the ship's deck. As a result, the captain was forced to push some of the containers over the side to prevent his ship from capsizing.

Aramco paid for the employee and his wife to go back to Houston for a week to buy all new furniture and household effects, and paid the cost of everything. He said it was quite a chore, finding and replacing everything on their inventory list in one week.

Living in Dhahran Hills made it necessary for Monica to have transportation to work, and for taking Blaine to and from the babysitters. Monica was allowed to drive in Dhahran—but couldn't drive outside camp—so she used the family private car for transportation. After living in Dhahran Hills for a few months, we got to know several neighbours with vehicles who travelled to Dhahran in the mornings. I could always get a ride if need be. If I didn't have my company truck for some reason, I could also get a Greyhound bus to work. It was provided to employees free of charge, and stopped almost outside our door at six forty in the morning. I could also get a bus home if need be.

Now that we lived in Dhahran Hills, I decided to buy Sid (illicit alcohol) once in a while.

"I've found a distributor," I told Monica, "and he lives in the Hills not far from us. I talked to him on the phone today, and he said it would cost three hundred and ninety riyals a gallon, that's about one hundred and thirty-five Canadian dollars. We have to cut it with a gallon of water, as it is almost pure alcohol, so we're actually getting two gallons."

That evening after dark, I drove to George's house with two half-gallon glass containers to pick up the Sid. I had phoned George just before leaving home to let him know that I was coming. I looked in all directions as I left the house to see if anyone was watching, or if there was anyone watching from a parked car. It felt like a covert operation. I glanced in the rear-view mirror to see if I was being followed as I drove to George's house. I felt a little nervous as I approached his house because I wondered if someone was watching. Most probably not, but I still had this uncomfortable feeling deep down inside. I drove into the driveway as close to the door as possible. It only took a few minutes for George to fill the containers and for me to pay him, and be back in my car and on the way home again. I still had this uncomfortable feeling. Perhaps it was the guilt of doing something that I knew was illegal, and not knowing if at any second a police car would come out of nowhere with lights flashing and stop me.

I felt a little easier after I was safely home, and the Sid tucked away at the back of a kitchen closet behind a number of canned foods and grocery products.

Most people drank Sid with tonic water and a twist of lime. It had a distinctive taste but resembled a gin and tonic, and if not cut with water would flame readily—similar to brandy.

One of my friends made an excellent Cointreau style orange liqueur. He made it by suspending an orange over a container of Sid. It turned out very close to the real thing. Over the years, many recipes were developed using Sid. These recipes were often passed down from long-time employees to the new hires.

After we moved into our new home, we had more room in which to entertain our friends. Monica had collected a number of new international recipes from Saudi, Indian and Philippine friends, and work associates, and was looking forward to trying them.

Our first guests were Pat and Colette Miller and their two girls, Alana and Sarah. Monica met Pat at the hospital when he came in for treatment on his shoulder. Pat had been making wine for several years and was getting quite proficient at making an excellent white. He had brought along a bottle for Monica and me to try. Just as we were sitting down to a glass of wine before supper, there was a knock at the door.

"I wonder who that could be," Monica exclaimed. "We're not expecting anyone."

She went into the hall to answer the door, and through the glass panel beside the door, she could see a Saudi standing there in his thobe and ghutra. Monica came back into the sitting room and suggested that I answer the door. As a precaution, we quickly hid our wine glasses in the bureau, and Pat poured his wine into a potted plant sitting on the coffee table. As I went to answer the door, I could see a Saudi in a white thobe and red checked ghutra through the narrow window that looked out over the entrance to the front door. It was unusual for a Saudi to be knocking at the door. The first thing that came into my mind was police! My heart started beating fast as I opened the door to the unknown Saudi, who looked very official to me. The first words out of the Saudi's mouth were, "How you all doing," in a strong Texas accent.

I was astounded, and couldn't help releasing a chuckle as I said, "Hi." He said he was selling fresh fish and shrimp, and wondered if we would like to buy some. Not knowing how fresh the fish would be, I said I didn't need any but thanked him for calling.

"How did you get an American accent?" I enquired.

"I went to school in Houston, when my parents lived in the United States, and spent most of my younger years there," he replied.

It was strange to hear him talk with such a Texas drawl, when his skin tone, features and dress were undoubtedly Saudi. He said he would be around again in a week or two but he never did call back again.

After he left, we all had a good laugh. The Saudi's voice had been heard in the living room by Pat, Colette and Monica.

"It's very unusual for a Saudi to call at the door selling something," Monica said. "I don't think that has happened before in the time we've been living on camp."

Monica often took Blaine for a walk around the neighbourhood and got to meet a number of the neighbours. The opposite side of our street was flat open desert where I could play soccer with Blaine. I piled rocks for the two goal posts, and Blaine would kick his soccer ball at the goal. It was generally too hot for Blaine to stay out very long running around, but it gave him some exercise and some time with me.

A new swimming pool had been built in Dhahran Hills. It was a lot larger than the one in Dhahran. Quite often Monica and Blaine would spend an hour or two at the pool, and I would meet them there after I finished work at four o'clock. Blaine attended a pre-school when he turned three. He really enjoyed it and looked forward to going, and made several new friends of his own age. As a result of the pre-school and children's parties organized by Monica's work friends, he got to know a number of children of his own age. The parents often organized fun events for the children.

Porter Danton, one of Aramco's personnel managers, lived next door to us in a house identical to our own. I had met him in the personnel department several times on work-related business. The last time being when I was arranging my daughter Jane's visit to the kingdom. He had gone to school and university in the United States, and had lived there most of his life, but had been born in Beirut, Lebanon. Not long after Monica and I moved into our new home, he came over and introduced himself and stopped for a cup of coffee. He was a pleasant man, tall, and well-built, with black curly hair.

"Typical personnel manager type," I had remarked to Monica.

It was a Friday afternoon that I'll always remember, and would relate many times over to friends as a funny story. My diving buddy Jim and his wife Fiona were visiting for the afternoon, and were staying for supper.

Monica was busy in the kitchen preparing dinner. I was in the living room relaxing with a home-made beer, which Jim had brought along for me to try, when the phone rang. Monica picked up the phone in the kitchen and shouted to me, "It's for you, Mark, Porter from next door."

"Hi Porter, how are you?" I replied as I picked up the phone.

"Hi Mark, I'm going on vacation back to the United States next week for three weeks. My wife left a week ago, and I have a young friend who'll be house sitting whilst we're away. I've something in the house that I don't want to leave here while I'm away. You can have it if you would like."

I immediately thought of alcohol of some description, and realised that Porter didn't want to mention it on the phone.

"I'll be right over," I replied.

When Porter answered the door, he explained to me that he had about ten bottles of red wine in storage, and said I could have all ten bottles. He was reluctant to leave them in the house. I was delighted as I didn't have any wine, and would now have wine for supper with our friends.

"The wine is upstairs in the return air vent," he explained to me, "so perhaps you could help me get it down and into the kitchen."

"Of course," I replied. "I'd be happy to."

When we entered the upstairs landing, I could see that Porter had taken out the four screws of the return air vent grill, and had removed the grill. He had it placed against the wall. Inside the vent were the bottles of wine.

"I've taken a few bottles downstairs to the kitchen already," Porter said.

I knelt down to reach into the return air duct, and noticed that the carpet was wet.

"Your carpet is wet, Porter."

"Yes, I know; I had a little accident with one of the bottles."

After several trips downstairs to the kitchen, we had all the bottles of red wine sitting on the kitchen countertop beside the sink. The kitchen table and most of the kitchen counters were covered in opened and unopened mail. It was obvious that since Porter's wife had left for the United States, he had been eating out. He hadn't done any tidying or filing of his mail. It seemed to have been left in a haphazard mess wherever he had opened it.

Most people bottled their wine in the bottles that the grape juice came in. The Dhahran commissary sold both red and white Rauch pure grape juice, and it was from this juice that Aramcons made wine by adding yeast. Almost an entire aisle in the commissary was dedicated to stocking the juice because it was so popular, and in high demand. The thirty-four ounce bottles had a wire flip-top similar to the old pop bottles of yesteryear. Many Aramcons also used them for bottling beer. Removing the flip-top cap could be dangerous if pressure built up in the bottle as many a user found to their misfortune. It was advisable to wrap a towel around the top when flipping the cap. If the bottle had excess pressure, it could result in the cap flipping over the bottle's neck and hitting your thumb. If the pressure was high enough, it had been known to take off the bottle neck as the cap flipped over and hit the neck. Many a brewer also had the bottles explode unexpectedly in the middle of the night due to excess pressure.

It was a very hot day. I realized that we would be taking the wine bottles from the air-conditioned house to the one-hundred-and-ten-degree temperature outside on the walk over to my house. The sudden temperature change could result in a bottle exploding if any of the bottles contained excess pressure from the yeast. Not wanting to risk that, I suggested to Porter that he relieve the pressure in the bottles before we carried them over. Porter agreed.

He took the first bottle and eased the flip-top off; there was a little pressure in the bottle but nothing excessive. Porter stood the bottle in the sink with the top opened. He proceeded to do the same with the second and third bottles. As he eased the top off the fourth bottle thinking that there would be next to no pressure, similar to the other three bottles, there was a sudden "pop." The flip-top sprang off violently, taking Porter by complete surprise. The contents of the bottle discharged rapidly like a fountain and hit the white stipple ceiling of the kitchen, spraying it with bright red wine. Red wine showered Porter and me as it dripped down from the ceiling, covering the mail that was strewn on the countertops and kitchen table. My white shirt was spotted with red, and streaks of red wine ran down our face. As Porter reacted to the fountain from the bottle, his elbow knocked one of the unopened bottles on the counter top, sending it into the sink with the three opened bottles. As the top of the bottle hit the sink, it dislodged the flip-top to one side, sending a fine spray of red wine across the kitchen. It hit the wall oven, spraying it with a mist of red wine. Porter quickly grabbed a towel and wrapped the bottle top to prevent it from spraying more wine.

"Oh my goodness!" I exclaimed. "We've got a real mess here now. How are we going to clean this wine off the ceiling?"

As I said that, the kitchen wall-phone rang. Porter snatched it up and said "Hello. Yes, he won't be long, Monica. He'll be back in a few minutes." And he returned the phone to its cradle. "That was your wife; she was wondering when you would be back."

"We better try to get this mess cleaned up," I said. "I don't know how we're going to clean your ceiling."

"Don't worry about it; I'll take care of it later. Let's get the rest of these bottles opened and get them over to your place."

Porter proceeded to open the remaining bottles, but this time he wrapped a towel around the flip-tops as he gingerly eased the tops off. Two more bottles had excess pressure in them, but the towel retained the spray, soaking the towel in red wine. After opening all the bottles and resealing them, we carried them over to my home. Porter had a horrendous mess to clean up, but refused to let me help. I changed my shirt and washed the red wine from my face, and felt a little more refreshed before sitting down to finish the beer that Jim had brought for me to try. After I told Jim about the problem Porter had with the wine, Jim thought the wine may not be that good to drink.

"It is probably still fermenting, and could give you a stomach ache," he said. "Why don't we try a glass and see how it tastes."

It didn't taste very good at all. Jim suggested that we put all the wine in a five gallon plastic container, that I had purchased to make wine, and put an air lock on it.

He thought that it had not finished fermenting, and may improve if it sat for a few days. "Sounds like a good idea; let's do it," I replied.

After pouring the wine into the five-gallon container, we noticed that most of the bottles had a layer of sludge at the bottom.

"I don't think Porter knows much about wine making," Jim commented. "I think you'll probably wind up throwing this wine down the drain. It may have bacteria in it, or some other problem; it doesn't look good to me."

The wine sat in the five-gallon container for three weeks, and didn't seem to improve. In the end, I decided that it wasn't worth risking a stomach problem, so I poured it down the drain. A sad end to Porter's red wine!

Floyd Harper at my office was telling me about the problems he was having with his Suzuki dirt bike. He had bought a box of bits from a 'For Sale Ad' he saw on the notice board at the mail centre. He had spent several weeks building the bike and getting it running.

"It's been sort of a hobby for me, Mark, something to do in the evenings rather than reading a book or watching TV."

Floyd was from Wales and was hired by Aramco on single status, as were all the Brits. Only the American and Canadian hires were allowed to bring their families. The Brits were paid to go back to England every eight weeks because they didn't have most of the benefits that the Americans and Canadians had.

"I'm thinking of selling the Suzuki, Mark. I don't think I'll ride it much so there is little point in keeping it."

"I may be interested in buying it if you do decide to sell it. Any idea how much you would want for it?"

"I'll think about it and let you know."

A week later Floyd told me he would sell the bike for five hundred riyals, and I decided to buy it.

"It is not running that well so you'll need to do a little work on it," Floyd said.

I had owned several fast road bikes back in England when I was an apprentice toolmaker at Westland Aircraft. Like many of my friends, I had a love for bikes when I was in my mid to late teens. I later traded my last bike, a five hundred Norton, for a Triumph TR2 sports car, and that's when my love of fast sports cars started. I moved on to MGB's and Jaguar 'E' Types.

There was a desert opposite our new home. I had noticed several dirt bikers riding on what appeared to be a track, about two hundred yards to the south.

Floyd was right about the bike not running very well. I replaced the spark plug, removed and cleaned the carburetor, and replaced some of the electrical wiring, after which it started much easier. I rode over to the track I had seen other bikers use, and not being an experienced dirt bike rider, I found it sufficiently challenging.

The Suzuki came to a sudden stop one day as I headed out on the track. Try as I might, I couldn't get it running again. Pushing it the quarter of a mile home was a hot job in the mid-morning sun, and I was about all in when I arrived home.

After a cool glass of lemonade in the air-conditioned kitchen with the Suzuki manual, I gained no insight as to what could be wrong. I had checked everything I could think of and was at a loss as to what could be amiss. The bike seemed very difficult to kickstart, almost as if it had partly seized. I decided I would change the oil in the sump as I didn't know if Floyd had changed it. When I released the drain plug with a catch pan underneath, I was alarmed to see what came out. The sump was full of a gasoline and oil mixture, and judging by the amount of fluid that came out, the sump must have been completely full. After flushing the sump with a thin flushing oil, and refilling it to its correct level with the appropriate grade of oil, it started easily and ran like a new bike.

No wonder it didn't run well, I thought.

It was trying to compress the fluid in the overfilled sump, which it couldn't do.

After that, I had no further problems with it, and enjoyed many an hour out in the desert in the dunes and on the track.

CHAPTER 20

Party Time

In 1933, Saudi King Abdel Aziz granted the Standard
Oil Company of California a concession to explore,
search and drill for oil in the country's vast Eastern
Province, an area about twice the size of Texas. Two
American geologists, Bert Miller and Krug Henry,
landed at the sleepy coastal village of Jubail and began
their search for oil.

In 1938, the company's gamble paid off. Its
geologists and drillers discovered oil in commercial
quantities at the Dammam Dome, near Dhahran.
Several wells were drilled but none produced oil in
sufficient quantity to be commercially viable, until well
No. 7 was drilled. "Lucky No. 7," as it came to be called,
(known as the stubborn well) is the mascot, the symbol
of first success.

The next year, Aramco exported its first tanker-load
of petroleum. Dammam No. 7 stands on a hill named
Jabal Dhahran, near a cluster of peaks called Umm
al-Rus. The partnership between Abdel Aziz's

government and Standard Oil became known as the Arabian American Oil Company (Aramco).

Texaco soon joined the partnership, and about a decade later, so did Standard Oil of New Jersey and Socony-Vacuum Oil.

In the early 1980s, after 45 years of nearly continuous output producing more than thirty million barrels of oil, Dammam No. 7 was taken out of production because of slack demand. However, the well is still capable of turning out about 1,800 barrels a day and as always, without a pump.

In 1983, Aramco celebrated its 50th anniversary.

As part of the celebration, King Fahd visited Saudi Aramco in Dhahran on Aramco's 50th Anniversary. He inaugurated the new Exploration and Petroleum Engineering Center (EXPEC), and the engineering building. It was a milestone in the company's operations. Aramco ran a ten-foot wide red carpet from the roadway and along the front of the EXPEC building up to the front entrance.

When the king arrived in his white Mercedes, his car drove slowly along the red carpet to the front entrance. He was followed by a crowd of well-wishers, photographers, police and the National Guard. He stepped from the car, gave a brief wave and entered the building to fulfil his royal obligations.

Dhahran is the site of the largest of Aramco's residential communities, and the company's administrative and technical headquarters. Dhahran has come a long way in fifty years. It grew from a group of huts in the desert, made of palm tree leaves with no electricity and no windows, to a modern residential community similar to a small California town.

Pipelines now criss-cross Saudi Arabia in a great network, transporting oil and gas to numerous Aramco facilities. Oil from the giant Ghawar field and the kingdom's southern fields is piped into the Abqaiq oil processing and crude stabilization facility. The resultant dry, hydrogen sulphide-free, stabilized oil is sent to the refining plants in Ras Tanura and Jubail on the east coast, and Yanbu on the west coast.

In the early 1980s, 60,000 people worked for Aramco at various locations across Saudi Arabia. More than a quarter of all the oil found on earth was found in Saudi Arabia and produced by Aramco.

Off the north-east coast of Saudi Arabia lies Safaniya, the largest offshore field in the world. Eighteen wells were put in production in 1957, flowing 50,000 barrels of oil per day. Ras Tanura lies 43 miles (70 km) north of Dhahran on the Arabian Gulf and is the site of Aramco's first refinery, and its largest oil-shipping terminal.

Ju'aymah, site of Aramco's second crude oil export terminal and gas fractionation plant, is located a few kilometres northwest of Ras Tanura. Udhailiyah, 118 miles (190 km) southwest of Dhahran, is the residential community for Southern Area Producing and the 'Uthmaniyah Gas Plant'. At Yanbu on the Red Sea, Aramco-operated facilities include a refinery, a crude oil export terminal, and a natural gas liquids (NGL) fractionation plant. Fractionation is the process by which important products for petrochemical industries are separated from natural gas, and then prepared for shipment to a variety of users.

Three gas processing plants at the Berri, Shedgum and Uthmaniyah oilfields were constructed under the Master Gas System. Berri was the first to come on stream, and was the forerunner of the massive gas plants in Shedgum and Uthmaniyah. It was officially opened by King Khalid in 1977. These plants gather and process the natural gas produced in association with crude oil for use in the kingdom's industrialization program. By the early 1980s, the system was producing and piping natural gas to petro-chemical plants and other industrial plants in the industrial cities at Jubail on the Gulf, and Yanbu on the Red Sea.

Using the natural gas as feedstock, the plants manufactured products that both fed other industrial operations and were exported. The natural gas collected by the master gas system was also used to generate electricity for urban and industrial use, to run desalination plants and to provide natural gas liquids for export abroad.

Aramco also constructed a number of gas-oil separation plants, called "GOSPs". Their function is to separate gas and water from crude oil, before the crude can be sent any distance through pipelines or manufactured into products. The oil goes to the Abqaiq Plant, and the associated gas goes to 'Uthmaniyah and Shedgum gas plants for further processing. The Abqaiq site stabilizes the oil, and then pumps it to Ras Tanura where it is exported or further refined.

In addition to all the petro-chemical facilities constructed throughout Saudi Arabia, Aramco also constructed schools, hospitals, residential compounds, housing, roads, bridges, shipping terminals, power plants and airports. Aramco has come a long way in fifty years. In addition to developing the oil industry, Aramco developed infrastructure, built numerous support manufacturing facilities and established training programs to replace foreign workers with Saudi nationals.

* * * * *

I had been working out of the portable buildings at Dhahran Heights up until this time. When the new engineering building was opened, the Vendor Inspection Division moved into the new building. Individual offices were arranged around the outside walls for managerial personnel on the floor that I was on. The centre space was divided into offices for two people with seven-foot-high soft surface portable acoustic panelling. After working out of a cramped portable building for several years, it was a refreshing change to be in a brand new building with modern facilities.

Many other engineering departments that were housed in various locations around Dhahran, were also moved into the new building. As a result, many of the project meetings that I attended were now held in the same building, saving a lot of time for all involved.

When expatriate personnel in our department go on vacation, and the British go quite often, someone has to cover their work when they're out of the kingdom. In addition to my normal work, I would often cover some of the workload of Floyd Harper, with whom I shared an office in the new building. Floyd was from Wales, and returned home about every six weeks for a short holiday. When Floyd was on leave, I monitored the construction of pressure vessels at a company in

Jubail, fibreglass pipe at a company in Dammam, and several other companies in Dammam and Al-Khobar.

More and more products were starting to be fabricated in the kingdom. A new company in the kingdom was required to have a Saudi partner with a 50 percent ownership in the company. My primary responsibility was monitoring the coating and welding of cross-country pipelines and undersea pipelines.

A new fabrication plant was set up to produce spiral wound pipe in the kingdom near Dhahran. Because of my knowledge and experience with pipelines, I was assigned the responsibility of monitoring fabrication and overseeing quality assurance at that plant.

George Dennison, plant manager of one of the companies that specialized in coating materials, decided that he would throw a party at his home in Dammam. The party was for his company employees, and Aramco employees involved with pipeline coating and construction. He was an American from Houston, and I had gotten to know him quite well. Monica and I were invited to the party, as were a number of project people from Aramco's pipeline groups.

George had a large home in the western suburbs of Dammam, which was part of the benefit package that came with his job. A high wall for privacy surrounded the home, like most large Saudi homes. There was a wrought-iron entrance gate at the curbside. The party was catered by a hotel in Al-Khobar, and was a goat grab. The goat grab is a traditional meal in Saudi Arabia. The goat had been pit barbecued and was the focal point of the serving table in George's large dining room, and the main dish of the meal. The goat was on a large silver platter on a bed of rice, with banana, raisins and tabouli (chopped tomatoes, onions, parsley and mint, olive oil, lemon juice and spices). Dates, oranges, pita bread, seeds, several vegetable dishes, pickles, yogurt, rolled grape leaves, hummus and traditional Saudi tea were also provided.

The meal is traditionally eaten with the fingers, by scooping up the rice in a ball and by pulling the hot meat off the carcass with your right hand. Don't eat with your left hand since the left hand is seen as the 'dirty hand'. Traditionally, guests, men and sons eat first, followed by the women and daughters. If there are non-family members present, the women and girls will likely have their own tray of meat and rice in a secluded room by themselves.

As all the guests were westerners, a row of forks were provided next to the goat platter for pulling off the goat meat rather than using your fingers. The meat was perfectly cooked and very tender, and could be pulled off very easily.

It was a really enjoyable meal, and the first goat grab that Monica and I had experienced. It was a good opportunity for Monica to meet other wives, and for me to socialize with people I normally only met in meetings discussing project matters. Alcohol wasn't provided. George didn't want someone leaving the party and having a problem on the way home.

It was the early hours of the morning when Monica and I left the party and drove home to Dhahran. We'd arranged for a babysitter, who was staying the night, to look after Blaine. Both were in bed when we arrived home.

* * * * *

Yanbu' al Bahr, known as Yanbu, translates to Spring by the Sea in Arabic. It was established thousands of years ago when early Egyptian traders crossed the Red Sea, then travelled on land routes into Jordan, to the north, and Jeddah, to the south. Originally, it was a staging point on the spice and incense route from Yemen to Egypt and the Mediterranean region. It is a little city located on the Red Sea coast of Saudi Arabia, in the Madinah Province, and is divided into three villages.

For many years, Yanbu was an insignificant Red Sea fishing port surrounded by an arid coastal plain.

The Yanbu Industrial City was developed under the direction of the Royal Commission for Jubail and Yanbu. Established in 1975, the commission was responsible for providing the entire infrastructure, both physical and social, needed to construct and operate the huge industrial developments at Jubail and Yanbu. The Yanbu Commercial Port is approximately 460 nautical miles south of the Suez Canal and 168 nautical miles northwest of Jeddah, and has storage facilities for all types of goods. It is a natural harbour, sheltered by the mainland to the north and east, and by coral reefs to the south and southeast. It is reached by a mile-long channel. Extending along 15 kilometres of coastline, King Fahd Industrial Port, Yanbu is the largest oil and petrochemical-exporting complex on the Red Sea. It was completed by the Royal Commission in 1982, and operated by the Saudi Arabian Seaports Authority since 1984. The port comprises seven terminals with 25 berths, a service harbour, bulk cargo and container handling equipment, and marine support facilities. The port handles crude oil from the

Eastern Province delivered through the east-west pipelines. The 1,202-kilometre (747 miles) pipeline and a natural gas liquids pipeline beside it carry oil and gas from the east to the west coast, to fuel and feed Yanbu's industries. The pipeline provides a Red Sea outlet for Saudi oil and reduces the kingdom's dependence on a single Gulf outlet. During the years, the crude oil terminal has pumped billions of barrels of oil destined for markets around the world. Dredged to a depth of 32 metres, the terminal consists of four loading berths connected to shore by a trestle and causeway. Two berths, which can be used concurrently, provide a maximum loading rate of 300,000 barrels per hour.

Yanbu Commercial Port is the nearest major Saudi seaport to Europe and North America, and is the focal point of the most rapidly growing area on the Red Sea. Traditionally, it has served as the nearest gateway for sea-borne pilgrims bound for the holy city of Madinah. Port expansion in 1979 increased the capacity to nine berths with modern facilities and equipment. It can handle in excess of three million tons of cargo per year. Yanbu Commercial Port played a major role in development of many refineries and project plants. In the early years, the port handled huge quantities of general cargo, project cargo, heavy lifts, containers and various construction materials (including bulk cement clinker). The construction of the new port facilities at Yanbu probably ranks as the greatest single item in the city's amazing transformation.

The Yanbu Refinery was established in 1979 as part of the Petromin projects. The Petromin Corporation (formed in 1968 by a Royal decree) is a privately owned Saudi Arabian corporation. The purpose of establishing the company was to provide lubricants to the Saudi market. The Yanbu Refinery became operational in 1983. It produces liquid petroleum gas (LPG), gasoline, jet fuel, diesel oil, fuel oil and lubricants.

I visited Yanbu several times during the construction of the refinery on project related matters, and to provide seminars on quality assurance for engineering and procurement personnel. The Aramco residential compound at Yanbu, which houses expatriate workers and their families, had an active scuba diving club. Among divers, the Red Sea is considered to have some of the best diving locations in the world. Diving at Yanbu is generally outstanding! The visibility, as well as the number and size of fish is normally better than Jeddah. Soft coral is abundant along the coast due to the strong currents. The main scuba diving location is an empty beach located north of Yanbu's creek.

The reef, consisting of a steeply sloping wall in most places, which goes down to around 100 feet or more before reaching a less steeply sloped sandy bottom. Occasionally, there are sandy shelves at between 30 and 70 feet. There are many cavern-like structures in the shallow areas at the top of the wall but they don't go very far back.

The sites, known as Barracuda Beach and Coral Gardens, have always been the favourites. Barracuda Beach is a deep area where barracuda are known to congregate, as well as tuna, sharks and other larger fish. Coral Gardens is a shallow area of sloping sand where corals bloom beautifully, and the current can be extremely swift. At the reef edge, it's about 15 feet deep—great for ending the dive.

The diving centre started out in 1980 as a club formed by a very small group of expatriate divers who'd come to Yanbu as engineers and construction workers.

They knew that the nearby Red Sea reefs were among the best diving sites in the world. Fortunately, some of those early members were qualified instructors. They began to pass their knowledge on to the other club members, similar to the club in Dhahran.

My diving buddy Jim and I made a trip to Yanbu one weekend with members of the Dhahran Diving Club. Many expatriate workers travel back and forward from Yanbu to Dhahran for various reasons including holiday trips, shopping and business. As a result, Aramco provided an aircraft that left Dhahran on a Wednesday afternoon to pick up people in Yanbu, and returned those passengers to Yanbu on Friday evening. Quite often there were a number of empty seats on this flight to Yanbu, and also on the return trip to Dhahran on the Friday evening. Aramco would allow dive club members to use any empty seats available free of charge. This made diving in the Red Sea at Yanbu very economical.

It was mid-September when Jim and I made our trip to Yanbu with eight other Dhahran Dive Club members. When we arrived at Yanbu, we were met at the small airport by four members of the Yanbu Dive Club. They transported us into the family camp to refill our diving cylinders using the club compressor. Our air cylinders had to be drained of air in order for them to be transported in the aircraft luggage compartment. We refilled our cylinders and loaded them into a pick-up truck along with a small portable compressor loaned by the Yanbu club. After refilling, we were driven to the camp commissary to get provisions, and then to the diving site on the beach about seven kilometres north of the cement plant.

By the time we arrived at the beach, the sun was already starting to drop over the horizon. It looked like a large red ball of fire, casting red and yellow streaks across the calm waters of the Red Sea.

"We better look sharp and get you all set up for the night," the Yanbu diver Sam remarked, "before the sun sets and leaves you in darkness. You only have about twenty minutes."

Jim had brought a two-man tent for us to sleep in. He quickly erected the tent, whilst I helped other divers collect firewood which was washed up at the high tide mark on the beach behind us. We soon had a good fire going which provided all the light we would need to get supper prepared. Sam got the small portable compressor set up in the low sand dunes behind our camp, and said he would return in the morning about 11:00 a.m.

Six tents were soon erected on the soft sand. A roaring fire, crackling away in the silence of the beach, was sending embers into the twilight of the evening sky.

A gentle breeze was blowing off the ocean giving a little respite from the ninety-five degree ambient temperature. Low waves broke over the coral wall about seventy-five yards from shore, and picked up a red glow from the setting sun as they rippled their way slowly to the beach.

When the fire died down a little, hot wood coals from the fire were placed under a barbecue frame and our supper of hotdogs and burgers was soon cooking. Fresh dates, apples, bananas and watermelon from the commissary were the dessert choices. Many stories were told around the fire that evening about previous dive trips in Saudi Arabia and around the world. By 11:30 p.m., most of the divers had turned in for the night with the intention of making an early start in the morning.

In the early hours of the morning, a wind picked up that flapped the tent and woke me up from a sound sleep. I looked at my watch and saw 2:15 a.m. The temperature had dropped significantly, which is typical in the desert, and I was glad of my warm sleeping bag. The breaking of the waves over the coral reef was a little louder now, and the rhythmic sound soon lulled me back to sleep.

As I dragged on my swimming trunks the next morning, I could hear someone preparing the fire for breakfast. Someone yelled, "Wake up you lazy land lubbers; breakfast will soon be up."

Jim crawled out of the tent right after me, and walked down to the water to feel the temperature. He splashed some water on his face to wake up.

"Another nice day in the desert," he exclaimed. "I could take a lot of this."

It seemed the seagulls had smelled the cooking and were circling the camp. They were walking nearby in search of a handout or a wasted morsel from a diver.

We all sat around eating breakfast and discussing our morning dive. As there was a light current from north to south, the general consensus was that it would be best to do a drift dive. We would go north on the beach for about a quarter of a mile before entering the water. Yanbu divers had also suggested this as a relaxing way to view the coral wall and the fish and creatures that made their home in it. If you plan it right, you could drift with the current and exit the water at the beach camp. Thereby saving you from lugging your diving equipment along the beach after you exit the water.

"Sounds like a good plan," Jim said.

It was about 8:00 a.m. when Jim and I checked and prepared our diving equipment, planned our dive, and made our way north up the beach for our first dive. We walked out in the shallow water to the edge of the reef, and carefully dropped over the edge of the sharp coral wall. We were very careful to avoid getting cut by the knife-like edges of the sharp coral. A cut could attract sharks, and we knew that sharks were common in these waters. The last thing we wanted was to provide a blood trail which could be fatal for us.

The drop over the wall was something like being suspended over the edge of a twenty-storey building. I had never experienced anything quite like it before. The water was so clear with visibility about 75 feet. It faded to a deep blue at the ocean floor. It took me a few moments to get used to the fact that I was suspended over the sheer drop-off of an almost vertical wall. I felt as if I could fall at any moment to the depths below. But I quickly realized that I was in control and that wouldn't happen. It was a strange sensation.

Jim gave me the thumbs up, and we descended slowly to 30 feet, hanging there for a time looking at the abundance of fish and creatures that inhabit the coral wall. Sponges and sea ferns of many colours clung to the wall, some waving in the gentle current. Large numbers of brightly coloured clownfish, surgeonfish, pilot fish, and yellow and black banner fish swam around us with many coming in very near to Jim and me for a close-up look. Moray eels poked their heads out of crevices in the coral wall as we floated past.

It was a fascinating array of marine life with the wide variety of colours. The wall seemed to be alive with activity. I was intrigued with the red and white zebra-striped lionfish which I hadn't seen before. If attacked, it delivers potent venom via its 18 needle-like dorsal fins (its only defence). Its sting is extremely painful to humans and can cause nausea and breathing difficulties, but is generally not fatal. I knew not to touch it.

Jim indicated that he wanted to go deeper, so we descended to 40 feet, and then to 65 feet.

The wall didn't seem to change much, but the colours seemed to change a little as the light from above was diminished. The current drifted us very slowly south which was our plan. It made the dive effortless as we slowly floated along taking in the magnificence that the reef displayed. As I looked towards the surface, I could see several small sharks gliding around a school of fish near the edge of the wall.

Hope they stay there, I thought.

We ascended to 30 feet again, and continued to drift for another 30 minutes. I checked my watch, which indicated that we'd been down for 45 minutes. We'd planned a decompression stop for five minutes at 10 feet just to be on the safe side. After the stop, we ascended to the surface to see that we were about 50 yards north of our camp.

It was a little tricky getting over the edge of the wall again. We waited for a wave and slight swell, and drifted back over the edge of the wall to shallow water inside the reef.

After returning to camp, Jim and I completed the post-dive information in our diving log:

Water temperature: 76 degrees Fahrenheit.
Maximum depth of dive: 65 feet.
Average depth: 40 feet.

Bottom time: 50 minutes.
Decompression: 10 feet for five minutes.
Time out of water: 9:25 a.m.
Total dive time: 60 minutes.

"That was an incredible dive," Jim remarked. "I've never seen anything quite like those colours and sea life before." I had to agree.

We sat and planned our next dive for the afternoon at about 1:00 p.m. after an early lunch. We planned to go a little further north this time, which would involve a longer walk and possibly a longer walk back to camp after exiting the water.

For the rest of the morning, we helped other divers with dive preparation and the filling of tanks with the portable compressor. Two members of the Yanbu Dive Club arrived at 10:45 a.m. as promised, and assisted with tank refilling.

A cooling breeze was coming off the ocean which made the 90-degree ambient temperature a little more tolerable.

After a light lunch of fruit, pita bread and cheese at 11:45 a.m., we relaxed for an hour and planned our next dive. This dive would be to a maximum depth of 30 feet which wouldn't involve a decompression stop. At 12:45 p.m. we were headed up the beach, and by 1:20 p.m. we dropped in over the coral wall. It was a little trickier this time as the wave height had increased to about two feet, and the water seemed a little shallower at the reef's edge. After clearing the reef's edge, I signalled to Jim, and we descended to 30 feet. The marine life seemed to be a little more abundant at this location for some reason, as another diver had noticed and advised us. We kept between the 20 and

30-foot depth, and swam a little more with the current, hoping we wouldn't have to walk very far to return to camp at our exit point. When we surfaced after 45 minutes, we were surprised to see that we were about 30 yards south of our camp. Getting back over the reef's edge seemed a little easier this time due to the increased wave height. As we floated ashore, I collected some small pieces of coral that had been broken from the reef and washed inland.

When we were filling out our diving log, I indicated under 'remarks' that I had trouble with my mask leaking. I wasn't sure of the reason for this but thought possibly I had some hair caught under the seal.

Post dive entry read:

Water temperature: 76 degrees Fahrenheit.
Maximum depth of dive: 30 feet.
Average depth: 20 feet.
Bottom time: 45 minutes.
Decompression: Nil.
Time out of water: 2:05 p.m.
Total dive time: 45 minutes.

That evening around the campfire after supper, we roasted marshmallows and related stories of our dives.

"The only thing missing here," Dave remarked, "is a couple of Budweisers. Why don't you run over to the liquor store and get a 12 pack, Jim!"

Everyone laughed.

Jim and I had to agree that it was probably the best day of diving either of us had ever had.

"It probably doesn't get better than this. I can see why they say Red Sea diving is reputed to be the best in the world," Jim said.

The next morning we made one last dive before packing up to return to the airport to catch our flight back to Dhahran. We were in the water by 9:30 a.m. and out again by 10:15 a.m. I made a note in my diving log that my mask leaked constantly during the dive. I didn't know the reason for it but made a note to get a new mask the next time we were back in Canada on repat.

We were all at the airport early, in plenty of time to catch our return flight. Camping on the beach was fun. However, I was looking forward to jumping into the shower when I returned home to wash off the salt that had accumulated on my skin. It felt like sandpaper.

As we sat waiting in the small terminal building for our aircraft to arrive from Dhahran, I wondered if I would ever return to Yanbu to dive again. It was a trip I would always remember and probably the best diving I would ever experience.

The small turbo prop arrived on time from Dhahran, and about twenty passengers filed down the aircraft steps onto the tarmac. After the aircraft was refuelled, the terminal PA system announced that we could commence boarding. We carried our diving equipment out to the waiting aircraft where a baggage handler stowed it in the aircraft's baggage compartment.

The informal experience of boarding a private aircraft was refreshing after all the security checks and procedures that are normally involved when flying internationally. We were asked to show our Aramco identification as we boarded, and then we proceeded down the aisle to open seating. There were very few passengers other than the divers. Within a few minutes we were taxiing down the runway and lifting off to the rhythmic whine of the turbo prop engines. I could see the Yanbu refinery and the construction camp as the aircraft gained altitude and circled to get its flight path back to Dhahran.

* * * * *

My involvement with pipeline manufacturing and construction, and the coating of both cross-country and undersea pipe was taking up most of my working hours. I had taken a number of Aramco sponsored courses and seminars, and became qualified with the National Association of Corrosion Engineers, NACE, as a corrosion technologist. I knew very little about pipeline corrosion and coatings when I first went to Arabia. I was an instrumentation technician, who'd specialized in electrical and instrumentation inspection and testing, and thought I was being hired to do the same type of work with Aramco. I remembered the words of Jim DeAngelo, whom I first shared an office with in Dhahran Heights, when I was initially assigned the job of overseeing the Al-Qahtani Pipe Coating Terminal, in Dammam:

"Go along with it Mark, Aramco will train you, send you to school and make you an expert."

Jim was right. That's exactly what Aramco did.

One of the companies I worked with in Dammam had a large workforce. Its workers were housed in small villas in a company compound in the suburbs of

232 SID DIQUI IS MY FRIEND

Dammam. It was similar to Aramco's compounds but on a much smaller scale. Many of the people living there were company employees with their wives and children, mostly from the United Kingdom and Europe. The compound was walled. It had a swimming pool, tennis court, and recreational facilities for the children that included a large hall and playground.

The owner of the company was a very wealthy Arab sheik. When I was visiting the company one Tuesday afternoon, the plant managing director called me into the office for a chat. He was from India and had worked for the company for many years. He was a very polite and likeable man. He had obviously contributed greatly to the prosperity of the company over the years, having worked his way up from a bookkeeper to his present position. He talked to me in generalities about the company, upcoming workload, and future growth and expansion of the company that was planned.

Then he said. "We're planning a dinner party at the company compound this Thursday evening, Mark, for all the Aramco pipeline people that the company is associated with. We would like to invite you and your wife to be our guests."

"We look forward to that," I replied. "What time will it be?"

"We would prefer that you didn't drive. We will have you picked up with one of our cars at about 7:00 p.m. if that would be convenient."

"That would be fine," I replied.

"When you would like to return home, your driver will be waiting to take you back to Dhahran."

I gave him my address and phone number, and advised him to call if the driver has a problem finding my home, or if something unexpected should happen.

I was a little surprised at the invitation. I thought it would be a good opportunity for Monica to meet some of my work associates and their wives whom she hadn't previously met. They were just names to her when I talked about my work.

I told Monica about the invitation that evening. She said she would ask her usual babysitter to stay over for the night to look after Blaine, as it would probably be very late when we returned home.

At 6:55 p.m. on Thursday evening when I looked out of our bedroom window toward the street, I noticed a large black sedan parked at the front of our house. The driver appeared to be sitting reading a book.

"I think our car and driver is here to pick us up for the dinner party," I shouted down the stairs.

Monica had given the babysitter an emergency number for friends on camp, in case she had a problem whilst we were away. It would be unlikely that she could reach us at the party. You always had to plan for the unexpected she would say, especially where children are concerned.

"If there is a phone available at the party, we'll phone to see if Blaine is OK," she advised our babysitter.

At 7:00 p.m. there was a knock on the door. I opened the door to find a tall man dressed in grey slacks and open-neck shirt. He said his name was Bashr, and that he had come to take us to the party. Monica and I followed him to the car where he opened the rear door for us to get in. When driving out of the Dhahran camp, vehicles aren't usually stopped at the security gate for a check. However coming in, all traffic, with the exception of Aramco vehicles with an identification number and logo on the side, is stopped, and the Aramco ID has to be shown. I wondered how the driver had gotten into the camp as he didn't have an Aramco ID.

The company organizing the party must have made some prior arrangement with the security gate; otherwise the driver would never have gotten in.

If you have influence in Saudi Arabia, anything is possible, I thought.

He was a careful driver, unlike many nationals, and he kept to the speed limits. When we reached Dammam, the car wound through a maze of back streets, then picked up a major artery for about two miles and then turned off to more side streets. I knew my way around Dammam a little, but was now hopelessly lost. Some of the homes we passed were in a bad state of repair, and others were large and surrounded by high walls, and were obviously owned by affluent people.

The car came to the end of a road, and to a small traffic circle, beyond which was the entrance to a compound. At the entrance was a small guardhouse with a barrier arm to prevent vehicle entry. As the car approached the barrier arm, a guard came out of the guardhouse and lifted the arm, and the car passed through into the compound. There were a number of small houses and villas scattered around the compound. It was a park-like setting with trees, grassed areas, a playground and paved roads. The car pulled up to a long single-storey building and stopped behind several other large sedans parked in the roadway. The driver got out and opened the rear door of the car for Monica and me to get out. He escorted us to a set of double doors and indicated for us to go through.

"When you would like to return home, please come out to the car and I'll be waiting to take you home," he said.

The doors opened into a large open area that appeared to be a recreation hall. A long table ran down the middle. It was loaded with food, providing a choice of dishes to suit just about anyone's appetite. At the head of the table, a large silver platter contained a pit-roasted goat, along with tabouli and fresh dates. Dinner plates, dessert plates, knives, forks, spoons and napkins were laid out near the goat platter. A local hotel had obviously catered this grand spread as all the food was professionally displayed.

When we arrived, about thirty people were standing around in small groups chatting and drinking. I recognized many of them from meetings I had attended with the pipeline groups. At one end of the hall, a small bar had been set up with a bartender in a short white coat.

Although alcohol is banned in Saudi Arabia, it was being served here; the choice was limited to gin, scotch and vodka. When we approached the bar, the bartender added ice cubes to two glasses and asked what we would like to drink. I asked for a scotch on the rocks, and Monica a gin and orange. It was like being back home again, it made us forget we were in Saudi Arabia.

As we sipped our drinks, more people were arriving. Most of the guests brought their wives along. Monica had chance to meet and chat with other people from Dhahran, and from some of the contractor compounds in Al-Khobar. I introduced Monica to many of the host company personnel, and they in turn introduced us to their wives.

There were lots of chairs against the walls around the outside of the hall. Some of the guests had already seated themselves with plates of food on their laps. The hall was air-conditioned so in spite of the fact that there were a lot of people, it wasn't uncomfortably hot. There seemed to be no shortage of alcohol at the bar. The Arab sheik who owned the company obviously had good connections.

To be drinking real alcohol was a welcome change from the illegal Sid which most people would drink at home on camp. It certainly helped to get the party going, and people socializing. If the police had raided the place, a lot of people would have gone to jail, but that wasn't likely to happen on a private compound. The dinner was first class with so many choices of dishes and desserts that we couldn't try them all. Most people sampled the goat. It was exceptionally tender with hardly any fat which is typical of goat meat.

One end of the hall was free from the dinner service, and provided a good space for dancing. Most of the guests were from the United States, Canada and Europe. As a result, the music was mostly pop music from those countries with lots of the Beatles and the Rolling Stones. As well there were Country and Western dance tunes from the United States.

At twelve thirty, Monica and I decided to leave. A few of the guests had already departed, and we didn't want to be too late back in case there was a problem with Blaine. It felt hot outside after leaving the air-conditioned hall. It would have been in the mid to low nineties at that time of the night, but we soon cooled off after finding our driver and entering his car. He must have started it earlier to cool it off in expectation of his trip back to Dhahran with us.

I had had lots to drink, and knew that I would suffer from a hangover in the morning. I had a little bit of an uncomfortable feeling as we were being driven home, worrying we might be stopped or get into an accident on the road home. The driver was very careful and courteous. It wasn't what he would do that could potentially cause a problem, but what some other careless driver would do to involve us in a collision. There were lots of bad drivers in Arabia who seemed to have no respect for the traffic rules and regulations, and other people's lives.

When we entered the Dhahran camp gates, we were stopped at the security gate by the guard. The driver spoke to the guard in Arabic, and we were asked for our identification cards, which we handed to the driver. The guard examined the cards, handed them back to the driver and waved us through.

The driver made his way through main camp and then took Rolling Hills Boulevard to Dhahran Hills. It was about one thirty by the time the car pulled up in front of our home. The house was dark except for the light over the front door, a good sign that all was well.

I had a nasty hangover the next morning at breakfast, and was thankful that it wasn't a workday.

"You look green," Monica said.

"I feel green," I replied. "For some reason it seems to affect me more than it does back home. Perhaps it is from dehydration from the heat."

This was the first of several parties that Monica and I were invited to by this company at their compound in Dammam. We always felt a little uneasy about going because alcohol was provided. The company always provided a car and driver; otherwise we wouldn't have attended. The buffet-style dinners were always catered by a local hotel and were always first class. It was a good chance to meet and socialize with work associates and their wives. So we accepted the invitations.

CHAPTER 21

End of the Line

On a Tuesday morning in late March, when I entered the office at 7:00 a.m., I knew something was wrong. People were standing around in small groups chatting with serious looks on their faces, instead of starting to prepare for the workday.

The first person I came across was Floyd Harper, who was leaning against the soft divider of his office doorway, talking to Lorne Isborne. "Hi guys," I greeted them. "What's up?"

"It's Austin," Lorne replied. "He's been arrested."

"Really," I exclaimed, "what for?"

"As far as we can determine, he's been distributing pornographic movies."

"It doesn't take much for the authorities to consider a movie pornographic," I replied. "A girl in a bikini will do it."

"According to Lorna, Austin's wife, it is a little bit more serious than that," Floyd replied. "We'll probably know more in a few days."

When videos were relatively new to Arabia, Austin Barton had set up a tape club. When he went back on vacation, he purchased three video recorders. He gave them to three friends, on the understanding that they would each record three movies a week from the TV. The movies would be shipped to the United States forces base just outside Dhahran. Austin had a contact at the base who agreed to receive them in his mail, provided he could watch them. This avoided any customs involvement. Austin built up a sizeable tape club in his home, but Aramco received a complaint from neighbours in the street where Austin lived. Apparently they couldn't park outside their homes after work, because of all the cars coming to pick up tapes from Austin. Aramco gave him notification to shut it down.

Austin got around the problem by selling three shares in his tape club for twelve thousand dollars each to three associates. Now that the club was split up into four separate locations, the parking problem was eliminated. Austin also received a royalty on each tape rented out. He continued to supply the three new shareholders with the nine new taped movies a week that he received from his friends in the United States.

About a week after Austin's arrest, Lorne Isborne went to visit him in the Al-Khobar jail where he was being held. Lorne took him some cigarettes, candy bars and bottled water. As he suspected, Austin didn't have access to any of these provisions in jail.

When Lorne returned, he gave the department an update on Austin's condition, and the charges against him.

When Austin sold the shares in his tape club, he started making and distributing porn movies to people on camp. Somehow, a young Saudi teenage boy had gotten access to one of the videos. The boy's father found out and reported it to the police. According to Austin, Saudi police carrying sub-machine guns burst into his house one evening when he was watching television with his wife, and arrested him. They ransacked his house for three hours, confiscating a television and videotapes, and took him into custody on charges that he was operating a pornographic film club. He said he was interrogated for several days, about allegations he belonged to a "sex club" that made X-rated pornographic movies. Lorne said the charges were very serious, and Austin's legal representative had advised him to expect a lengthy jail term.

Lorne said the conditions in which Austin was being held were degrading, filthy and primitive compared to western standards. His cell was very hot with no air conditioning and little ventilation. He had a hard wooden platform for a bed with one blanket that Aramco had provided. He shared the cell with four other prisoners. There was a hole in the ground of his cell for a toilet. Austin said he had been beaten on the feet with a splintered stick, and he was beaten on the kidneys with a rubber riot stick and spat upon. He said the guards made sexual advances with the implication that by giving them his body, he would be freed. He said Austin considered suicide but couldn't find a way to do it.

His prison clothes consisted of only a pair of pajama bottoms. He was allowed to shower once a week, and if Aramco didn't bring him food, he would starve to death. Austin stated that the only food provided was rice dotted with "cooked cockroaches". He really appreciated the provisions that Lorne had taken him.

This was the first of several visits that Lorne made to the jail to assist Austin as best he could. Lorne said it was depressing to see him being held in those conditions. As time went on, Lorne said that Austin was looking sick and gaunt. He was concerned that his health was suffering badly as a result of the squalid conditions in the jail. He was also starting to get sores on his arms and face, probably due to the filthy conditions in his cell. He told Lorne that when they threatened to jail his wife Lorna if he didn't confess, he signed several confessions none of which were true.

A rumour spread around Dhahran that a British nurse had been into the clinic asking to have a butterfly tattoo removed from her buttock. She was afraid that she could be identified from one of the porno movies which had been confiscated from Austin's house.

From time to time, rumours are rife around Dhahran but there is generally some basic truth to them.

In Saudi Arabia justice is fairly swift. Within about two months a trial date was set, and Austin's case came before the judicial system.

Saudi Arabia is one of a number of countries in the world with judicial corporal punishment. In Saudi Arabia, this may include amputation of hands or feet for robbery, and flogging for crimes such as sexual deviance and drunkenness. The number of lashes is not clearly prescribed by law, and is varied according to the discretion of the judges. It ranges from dozens of lashes to several hundreds, usually applied over a period of weeks or months. It also includes stoning to death for adultery.

Austin had legal representation, and an interpreter so that he knew what was going on at his hearing. When his case concluded on July fourth, he was sentenced to three years in prison, and was fined the equivalent of one hundred thousand dollars. It was a harsh sentence but could have been a lot worse.

For some strange reason, Austin's wife Lorna was allowed to stay in their rental home on camp following his incarceration. She also continued her part-time employment at the Dhahran hospital. Normally, when the primary employee is not able to support the family, the family is immediately shipped home. Rumour had it that she was involved with a high-powered friend, a Saudi sheik, who pulled a few strings within Aramco so that she could stay.

Austin decided he would appeal his sentence and hired a young United States attorney that he knew, who also worked for Aramco in Dhahran. The attorney was confident he could get Austin out of jail. Within a couple of months his hearing was scheduled, but it didn't go in his favour. The court decided that at his first hearing he didn't get enough of a jail term, and they sentenced him to another year in prison. He was also fined the equivalent of another forty thousand dollars. Austin was devastated. He couldn't believe what had happened to him. His health was already starting to suffer. He thought he wouldn't be able to survive the four-year term he now faced. He felt it was the end of the line for him.

Austin served just over 17 months in prison. He was released on a King's pardon. It came on the day that Muslims began the annual hajj pilgrimage, as two million faithful set off from Mecca to the valley of Mina in Saudi Arabia.

The King often grants a pardon to some prisoners at this time of the year, and Austin was lucky enough to be one of them. Murderers never get pardoned.

Austin was 56 years of age when he was released, and was so weak he was unable to fly back to the United States. He was about 150 pounds when he entered prison, and had lost nearly 30 pounds. His relatives flew him to Cyprus, where he spent time recuperating and gaining strength before he was fit enough to make the long trip back home to New Orleans.

He was an engineer who'd gone to Saudi Arabia with his family. He wanted to make the extra money and receive the benefits that came with overseas employment in the harsh conditions of the Middle East. Not being satisfied by the good salary that Aramco paid him, he had embarked on an illegal moneymaking venture spurred by greed and visions of grandeur. Austin's legal costs and fines would have consumed a lot of the money he had saved from his Aramco salary and illegal tape club. He most likely left Saudi Arabia with a lot of ill feelings toward the authorities, and Aramco. Saudi Arabia wasn't a good memory for him.

Several years later, news articles appeared in United States newspapers and magazines in which Austin was featured and quoted. He claimed that in his job as an inspector, he had to reject a considerable amount of construction equipment that didn't meet specification requirements. He claimed the rejections cost Saudi officials a lot of money because of lost commissions which had resulted in his imprisonment.

Aramco subsequently took exception to Austin's allegations concerning the terms of his imprisonment while in Saudi Arabia. Aramco indicated that his claim—that the arrest stemmed from an engineering report criticizing the safety of an offshore rig—was baseless.

Aramco indicated that there is absolutely no connection between any report written by Mr. Barton and his subsequent arrest. There is nothing in either the Saudi police or court records that would lend any credence to his claim.

Having worked with Austin for several years, sharing an office with him and socializing from time to time, I knew exactly why Austin landed himself in jail. I knew that it had nothing to do with rejecting construction equipment as claimed by him. Austin only had himself, his greed and arrogance to blame for his eventual downfall.

CHAPTER 22

The Camel Market in Hofuf

Monica and I met the Aramco Greyhound bus in the parking lot just outside the mail centre. Friends Pat and Colette Miller were already on the bus. Blaine was left with a babysitter for the day. We thought it would be too long a day for him as we had to leave Dhahran for Hofuf at seven in the morning. Also too hot for him all day in the June sunshine.

The bus left on time but the lady who organized the trip didn't arrive, and the bus left without her. It was fortunate that the Filipino driver had been given detailed instructions and an itinerary, and knew where to go. He had made the trip several times before with other Aramco groups.

The bus trip to Hofuf took two hours but the bus was air-conditioned and a movie was provided, so the time passed quite quickly.

The town of Hofuf in the Ash Sharqiyah province, with a population of over 150,000, is located in the middle of the great Al-Hasa Oasis. The Al-Hasa Oasis is the largest and most important oasis in all of Saudi Arabia, and is a leading producer of dates. It has a large camel market each Thursday where you can find racing camels. It is visited by most Aramco employees at least once during their stay in Saudi Arabia. Hofuf is located inland, southwest of Abqaiq, and is the closest city to the famous Gahwar field, one of the world's largest conventional land-based oil fields.

Legend places this as the burial place of Laila and Majnoon, the star-crossed pair of the most popular love story in the Arab and Muslim world. The Queen of Sheba is also fabled to have visited this city from her kingdom in Yemen.

Hofuf also has one of the most interesting souks in the kingdom. Because of the enormity of the oasis, there are a number of picturesque villages scattered throughout its central oasis. Al-Hasa boasts two million palm trees. On the eastern side of the oasis is Jabal Qara, containing limestone caves named Ghar Al Hashshab 'cave of the arrow maker'. The caves are very cool, and are popular in hot weather. Around the Jebel are potters making simple unglazed pottery.

The Judas cave is located in this area, and is well worth a visit. A story tells how the Judas Cave was named after Judas Iscariot, one of the twelve apostle of Jesus Christ. After accepting the bribe of thirty gold coins and running away to cover his betrayal from his master, he holed up in this cavern.

The Al-Hasa region derives its name from the oasis at its centre. The region is bounded on the north by Kuwait, on the east by the Persian Gulf, on the south by the desert Rub al-Khali, or Empty Quarter, and on the west by the Dahnā sand belt.

Most of the population is congregated in Al-Hofuf and Al-Mubarraz. The rest of the population is scattered through more than 50 small villages, or is nomadic.

When the bus arrived at the camel market, the driver advised us that we had one hour before the bus departed for a lunch stop at a local park.

Camels have a certain fascination for most people. Maybe it's because of their strange ability to go without water for long periods of time, or perhaps it's because they look gawky and unlike most other animals. Or, perhaps it's because they're so deeply associated with the mysterious East: the land of sand, sheiks and camels! They tend to slobber a lot, are smelly disgusting animals for the most part, and are known to spit sometimes.

The market is located several miles outside the wonderful greenery of the oasis, in a flat barren desert area with a mish-mash of portable corrals. A mixture of large trucks, pick-up trucks, cars and—camel dung— are typical on market day. I estimated that there must have been several hundred camels at the auction, camels of every size, shape, age and colour. There seemed to be constant noise from people shouting and bargaining; vehicle engines and horns with the process of loading and unloading the camels; and camels snorting and bleating.

Many of the camel owners at the market were friendly and were willing to pose with their animals. They were generally accommodating of our unspoken requests for better photos, or photos with them.

I had a Miranda single lens reflex camera, which had both an eye-level and waist-level viewfinder. With the waist-level viewfinder, I was able to get shots of some of the Saudi women without them realizing that they were being photographed. I also had a video camera.

After wandering around watching the live auction, we came across a group of men preparing to put a camel into the back of a Datsun pick-up truck. Anyone who has ever been in Arabia has seen at least one camel tucked into the back of a pick-up truck. The camel sits facing backwards as the truck precariously drives down the highway, sitting on collapsed springs from the weight of the animal. To put the camel in, they generally back up the pick-up to a sand berm, and back the camel into the truck. The camels tend to spit, snort, grunt and complain a lot during the process—a very unwilling participant. Eventually the animal backs in and sits down. I had seen as many as three camels in the back of a pick-up truck.

Camels smell bad. Not just that dung smell you associate with animals, but they have a really horrible bad breath smell that permeates everything. Most of the camels weren't hobbled and seemed to be allowed to wander as they pleased. The owners will usually brand their camels on the neck with a distinctive marking as a means of identification and proof of ownership. The brand appears to be put on with henna, rather than being burnt into the animal with a hot iron.

I took lots of photographs, and also a lengthy video film of the camels that ranged in colour from a light brown to almost black. A camel had recently given birth, and the newborn was flopping on the ground looking like a drowned creature from another planet. There were also a number of cows at the market of several different breeds that could have been Guernsey and Friesian.

"Go stand beside that donkey cart," I said to Monica, "and I'll take your picture."

The cart looked like a relic from the past with wooden spoke wheels, and looked as tired as the donkey hitched to it. The donkey was like a pillar of stone and made no effort to move as Monica stood next to him.

The hour passed quickly, and it was soon time to get back on the bus for the trip to the park, and our packed lunch. It was refreshing to get back on the air-conditioned bus, after being in the hot sun for an hour with no shade and several hundred smelly camels.

The bus made its way through the crowded old streets and market areas of Hofuf. Many of the streets were heavy with traffic and pedestrians, and there was a constant hubbub of vehicle horns of impatient drivers. Many of the buildings looked old, as if they were left over from ancient times and in need of repair.

Hofuf was the capital of the Eastern Province until 1953. Various parts of the old town still show evidence of when the Ottoman Empire controlled most of the area. It has several landmarks of its recent distinguished past. Hofuf contains an old Turkish fort which has a large domed mosque within the walls. The mosque was believed to have been built by Ibrahim Pasha, the destroyer of Diriyah, in the 19th century. The fort itself was built in 1551 by the Turkish army.

The bus stopped by the rugged old walls of the Turkish fort. The fort stood tall today in the noon-day sun, in spite of the fact that it is more than 400 years old. A grand tribute to the builders of the time. I walked across the dusty street and snapped a few pictures of the fort, and took some video film. The dome of the old mosque could be seen jutting just above the high brown sandy walls of the fort.

The bus made its way, out of the main town of Hofuf, along a wide divided boulevard to an area of several small villages which were heavily treed with date palms. Beside the road, an irrigation trough ran for several miles providing the much-needed water for the otherwise dry parched sandy soil. The bus stopped at a heavily treed park for a picnic lunch.

Everyone was glad to relax under the coolness and shade of the eucalyptus trees, known locally as gum trees.

Pat Miller went exploring with his video camera as Monica and Colette spread a rug on the ground and prepared our lunch.

Pat soon came back and said, "Hey you guys, there's a swimming pool over there by that building. Not the type of pool you're used to but there are several kids in it splashing around."

I could hear the 'clack-clack-clack' of a water pump in the distance which was probably part of the irrigation system, or a pump for the pool. After lunch, we wandered over to look at the pool that Pat had found, and watched the Saudi kids splashing around enjoying themselves. Pat was right about the pool. It was in a rudimentary building. It was open at both ends, and had a sunshade roof under which was an above-ground concrete pool about twelve feet square. The water looked clean, and the kids in their white thobes were splashing around in the pool, and really enjoying themselves. That was all that mattered.

"You going in?" Pat asked Colette.

"You're kidding me," she replied. "You can try it Pat. We'll watch and take pictures of you if you like."

We watched for a while, and then went back to pack up our belongings before climbing aboard the bus. The bus was slowly filling up with passengers for our onward journey to Jabal Qara, and the potters cave and Judas cave.

Jabal Qara is one of the most prominent natural attractions away from the central oasis, and town of Hofuf. It is located approximately 13 km east of Hofuf, and consists of sedimentary rock formations, and natural caves with a distinct climate. It is not just a unique configuration of rocky outcrop; contrary to the prevailing atmosphere of the weather outside, these mountain caves are cool in summer and warm in winter.

The bus pulled into a sandy parking area to let all the passengers out. The driver gave instructions to be back at 3:15 p.m. for our journey home.

A wide sandy path between huge boulders and tall limestone formations led to a shallow cave where a potter was hard at work, making traditional Saudi pots. It was cool in the cave. About thirty people crowded around to watch the potter at work. The potter sat behind a rocky bench operating a wheel with a foot treadle. Not a word was spoken as he formed the pot from the lump of clay on his wheel. It took him about fifteen minutes to form the pot he was making. Then he stood up by his bench, as everyone clapped and filed out.

Outside the cave entrance, a variety of pots were on display on an old wooden platform supported by two large boulders, and many more were on the ground. They were all unglazed and, therefore, wouldn't hold water, but would be good for decoration and a memento of the area.

Pat and I each bought a small pot for ten riyals each which wasn't expensive considering the amount of time required to make them. There weren't many pots left after everyone had made a purchase.

The walk to the Judas cave was along a concrete pathway which led between towering rock formations of sandstone and huge boulders. Inside the entrance of the towering rock fissure, walkways and iron railings had been constructed so that the public could enter safely. The high walls of this cave, coupled with the cool limestone walls and gentle breezes, created an unusually soothing atmosphere on this hot day. The huge fissure funnelled air from above. The air seemed to lose heat on the limestone walls on its descent to the cave floor. It resulted in a welcome cooling breeze, and a respite from the heat.

We made our way through the fissure along a path that narrowed considerably in places. We came across an area where the sun was shining through the top of the fissure to the floor below. It projected a beam of light almost like a laser beam. It was quite an unusual sight. It lit up the cave floor in a pool of brightness but didn't seem to contain any heat.

The natives called it "Cabal Garra", which means a village of Green Mountain. They say there's a mystery that lies within this cave. The indigenous population believed that whoever hears the sighing of Judas and clanking of gold coins inside the cave will betray somebody dearest to his or her heart.

The sun felt burning hot as we made our way out of the coolness of the cave and back to the bus for the trip back to Dhahran. The driver put on another movie for the drive home. I noticed that many of the passengers were taking the opportunity to catch a nap as the bus headed back to the main highway to Dhahran.

CHAPTER 23

The Way Home

I was sitting in the office one afternoon, relaxing with a cup of coffee on my coffee break. I had recently received a letter from the people renting our home in Calgary. It indicated that the husband was retiring in a month and they would be moving to Vancouver Island. The couple were excellent tenants, and had been in our home since we left for Saudi Arabia.

Monica, Blaine and I had been in Saudi Arabia for five-and-a-half years, and Blaine had spent all his young life there. I had started work with Aramco when Blaine was four months old.

Perhaps this would be a good time to go home, I thought.

My biggest concern about being in the kingdom was getting into a traffic accident. I had never so much as had a fender bender during my five-and-a-half years, and I had done lots of travelling for my job. I credited my good record in part to being a defensive driver, and in part to good luck. How long could my luck hold out?

In addition, I thought that five-and-a-half years in a land of many restrictions for myself and my family was perhaps long enough. Our home was paid off several years ago. We'd managed to save and make good investments during our stay, which included the purchase of a second home on a lake east of Edmonton.

Why stay, I thought.

I had essentially reached my goals. When I returned home from work, I sat down with Blaine in the family room watching the television as Monica prepared our supper. I thought about it some more, and decided it was time to go back to Canada. After supper, when I asked Monica if she would like to leave Arabia, she said, "Sure, I'm ready to go home." It didn't take her any time at all to think about it.

"Would you like to go home to Canada?" she asked Blaine.

"For a holiday?" he asked.

"No, we'll leave Arabia and go home for good," she replied.

"But this is home, I only want to go for a holiday mummy."

Blaine had never known anything but Arabia. As far as he was concerned, this was where he went to school and grew up. He was already home.

I handed in my one-month written notice to Aramco after thinking about it for the weekend, and deciding that I had made the right decision.

Aramco is very efficient at both shipping you out to Arabia, and shipping you home again.

Monica and I spent the next few evenings filling out inventory forms, and deciding on what would go in our air shipment allotment, and what would go by sea freight.

I sold my motorcycle and my car, and apart from that, everything was shipped home. This included furniture we'd purchased in the United States, Hong Kong and the Philippines.

We had had a number of good holidays whilst being in Arabia, including a 49-day trip around the world that included Canada, Hawaii, Fiji, New Zealand, Australia, Singapore and Malaysia.

We'd also made separate trips to Thailand, Hong Kong, Cyprus, Egypt, the Philippines and Greece. Lots of great memories to look back on.

When our final flight from Saudi Arabia took off from the Dhahran airport, I looked down on the dusty desert landscape for the last time. I realized that I would probably never come back again to this land of oil wells and vast oil reserves. But never is a long time.

For me, it was a land of opportunity and career development. I had come to Aramco as an instrumentation technician, and returned home a certified corrosion technologist. I remembered once again the words of Jim DeAngelo (that seemed so long ago). Jim met us at the airport when we first arrived in Saudi Arabia, and later became a good friend and office partner.

"Aramco will send you to school, and make you an expert," and that's exactly what they did.

I felt sad to leave for many reasons: leaving the many friends we'd made, the beautiful home in the Hills and casual lifestyle, but I felt my time was up and it was time to return to Canada.

We flew to London, England, and rented a car and drove to Plymouth, Devon, to visit my cousin Noreen and her husband Tony.

We spent a week in Plymouth, and then, with Noreen and Tony and my daughter Jane, we flew to the Island of Majorca. We rented two old refurbished farm houses for a week each, both with their own private swimming pools. We spent time exploring the little towns on the island and relaxing on the sandy beaches. We hiked in the rugged hills, played around in the pool with Blaine, barbecued our suppers, and enjoyed the warm summer evenings with a bottle of local wine. It was a relaxing unrestricted freedom that wasn't available in Saudi Arabia.

We spent a further week in Plymouth when we returned to England two wonderful weeks later. Our flight back to Calgary brought a five-and-a-half-year adventure in a foreign land to an end.

Thank you Saudi Arabia, and Aramco. They were good years; we'll never forget them.

In memory of my friend, Jim.

32399054R00167

Made in the USA
Charleston, SC
18 August 2014